Managing Archival and Manuscript Repositories

**by Thomas Wilsted
and William Nolte**

The Society of American Archivists

Chicago

1991

© 1991 Society of American Archivists
        600 S. Federal, Suite 504
        Chicago, Illinois 60605

ISBN 0-931828-78-3

TABLE OF CONTENTS

Preface

Like the Basic Manual Series that precede them, and that for more than a dozen years excelled in articulating and advancing archival knowledge and skills, the seven new titles in SAA's Archival Fundamentals Series have been conceived and written to be a foundation for modern archival theory and practice. They too are intended for a *general* audience within the archival profession and should have widespread application within the profession. They will strengthen and augment the knowledge and skills of archivists, general practitioners and specialists alike, who are performing a wide range of archival duties in all types of archival and manuscript repositories.

From the beginning, these titles have been designed to encompass the basic archival functions enumerated by SAA's Guidelines for Graduate Archival Education. They discuss the theoretical principles that underlie archival practice, the functions and activities that are common within the archival profession, and the techniques that represent the best of current practice. They give practical advice for today's practitioners, enabling them to prepare for the challenges of rapid change within the archival profession.

Together with more specialized manuals also available from SAA, the Archival Fundamentals Series should form the core of any archivist's working library. The series has particular value for newcomers to the profession, including students, who wish to have a broad overview of archival work and an in-depth treatment of its major components. The volumes in the series will also serve as invaluable guides and reference works for more experienced archivists, especially in working with new staff members, volunteers, and others. It is our hope that the Archival Fundamentals Series will be a benchmark in the archival literature for many years to come.

Preparing these publications has been a collaborative effort. The authors have contributed the most, of course, but SAA readers, reviewers, staff members, and Editorial Board members have also assisted greatly. I would particularly like to thank Donn Neal, former Executive Director, and Susan Grigg, Chair of the Editorial Board, whose good counsel and support never failed; and Roger Fromm, Photographic Editor, and Teresa Brinati, Managing Editor, who brought the volumes from text to publication.

In addition, the Society expresses its deep appreciation to the National Historical Publications and Records Commission, which funded the preparation and initial printing of the series.

Mary Jo Pugh, Editor
Archival Fundamentals Series

Introductory Note

This volume seeks to provide archivists with an introduction to the concepts and functions of modern management. It will not substitute for a degree from the Harvard Business School; it will barely address, let alone explore, major areas of interest to the archival manager. The authors nonetheless hope that its presence in the Archival Fundamentals Series will alert archivists, including those beginning their careers, to the need to consider management responsibilities as an inevitable part of the operation of any repository, and management skills as essential tools in the successful direction of such repositories.

Over the last forty years, management studies have become increasingly quantitative, as anyone who might choose to search through back issues of the *Annals* of the Academy of Management would soon discover. The emphasis in this manual, however, is not on management science, but on applied management: the use of management techniques to enhance the performance of organizations, in this case archives and related repositories.

In preparing this volume, the authors have drawn on very different backgrounds. One has been an archivist and manager in private institutional archives and manuscript repositories; the other has been a historian and manager in the federal government. Their goal has been to bring useful perspectives from both sets of experience to this project. Though they have cooperated on the outline and focus of the manual, they have each assumed principal responsibility for individual chapters, resulting in the somewhat diverse styles that follow.[1] They hope the differences in style and emphasis will not be a distraction, but will point instead to the essentially pragmatic nature of management, where accomplishing objectives is more important than following a prescribed path to the defined goal.

Management is a skill, and enhancing it requires both practice and instruction. This manual will be successful if it provides archival managers, especially those with little formal training in management, with a better understanding of the management process and an introduction to basic tools that may prove useful in discharging their managerial responsibilities.

The authors are indebted to a number of individuals who assisted them in completing this manual. These include: Series Editor Mary Jo Pugh, Managing Editor Teresa Brinati, and the unnamed reviewers who made so many useful suggestions. The authors also extend special thanks to their wives, Mary Wilsted and Joan Nolte, for their assistance and forebearance through the many months of research and writing that went into this volume.

---

[1] Thomas Wilsted is the principal author of "The Archivist as Manager," "Organizational Structure," "Planning," "Fund Raising and Development," "Managing Archival Facilities," and "Public Relations." William Nolte is principally responsible for "The Management Process," "Human Resources: Dealing with People on the Job," "Financial Management," and "Technology and the Archival Manager," as well as the guide to management and professional associations.

Chapter 1

The Management Process

Introduction to Management

"Management" and its synonym "administration" are familiar words to archivists, almost always referring to the application of the principles of archival and records management to particular collections or bodies of records.[1] This manual will focus instead on the management of archival institutions and the application of the principles and techniques of management science and practice, as used by organizations in both the public and private sectors, to archives and manuscript repositories. The chapters that follow concentrate on the human, financial, and physical resources needed to care for archival holdings and on the basic functions (planning, organizing, budgeting, etc.) that must be performed to use those resources effectively. One purpose of this manual is to provide archivists with an introduction to the principles of management and to the literature of management science and practice.

"But I'm not a manager; I'm an archivist," the reader may say. Experience suggests that this reaction can be translated in several ways. First, the reader now finds himself or herself in a managerial or supervisory position, but prefers to see this as temporary or ancillary. For whatever reasons, the archivist, having devoted years to establishing a professional identity, may be reluctant to accept a different—and possibly unattractive—identity. Archivists-turned-managers may also sense the imbalance

between their extensive education and training in archives and related disciplines and their lack of commensurate managerial education.

This phenomenon is not unique to archivists. As noted by a former president of the American Management Associations:

> Most of us who practice management started out by doing something else. Some were engineers, others salespeople, [but] later the challenge of management arose and suddenly there was a need to learn a new profession.[2]

The increasingly organizational nature of modern society means that many professionals find themselves in career paths that frequently lead away from their technical or professional specialty and into management. Archivists, working in organizations and responsible for the records of organizations, cannot escape the managerial implications of their profession. At some point in their careers most archivists will find themselves performing managerial tasks.

"But I work in a one-person repository," others may say, exempting themselves from management functions, which, they assume, apply only to larger institutions. Not so fast. Though "getting work done through others" is a common definition of management, the circumstances of the archival community, where small institutions predominate, require a different definition. *Management is the exercise of re-*

---

[1] Though sometimes used to distinguish different levels of authority and responsibility, "management" and "administration" will, in this manual, be used synonymously.

[2] Thomas R. Horton, cited in William K. Fallon, ed., *AMA Management Handbook*, 2d ed. (New York: AMACOM, 1983), p. xi.

sponsibility for the effective use of the human, financial, and other resources available to meet an organization's objectives. If this definition is accepted, the lone curator clearly becomes a manager. Who else is available to plan and direct the use of the repository's resources? In fact, running a one-person archives is not a wise career choice for the archivist who wishes to avoid managerial responsibilities. Moreover, small institutions, though they may lack organization charts, complicated planning documents, and multivolume sets of internal regulations, need effective management on the part of their one- or two-person staffs. They simply have no margin of resources to spare.

A second objective of this manual is to acquaint archivists with the managerial culture. Archivists frequently complain that their managers (or resource allocators) do not understand them. It is no less true that archivists do not understand their managers. At the very least, a better understanding of managerial values, concepts, and terminology may assist archivists in communicating with resource allocators. On this point we should be candid: the gap in understanding between the two threatens archivists far more than it does their managers.

Finally, a better understanding of management may help archivists understand and document the structure and activities of their parent organizations and prepare the archival profession to deal with rapid changes in institutions and technology. In both public and private sectors, the science and practice of management accepts change as a virtual given, and emphasizes the manager's role in keeping an organization in touch with fluctuations in its operating environment.

Modern Management

Conscious attention to management began in the late nineteenth century, with the development of the corporation as a new form of social organization, larger and more complex than all but a few predecessors. By the early twentieth century, several attempts at defining "scientific management" had appeared. Chief among these were the works of the American Frederick W. Taylor, whose time studies were applied mostly to industrial situations. The Belgian Henri Fayol, whose works overlap Taylor's in many respects, went beyond the industrial setting to suggest that scientific management could be applied to other situations as well. Fayol's work, along with early studies of bureaucracy by Max Weber, laid the basis for much of what has followed in management and related fields.

Fayol suggested that all management actions could be reduced to one of five basic functions: planning, organizing, budgeting, directing, and controlling. Subsequent work has added functions (e.g., communicating and coordinating) and softened some of Fayol's terms, giving a more democratic quality to terms which may have sounded authoritarian. "Directing," for example, is now commonly replaced by "motivating." Nonetheless, Fayol's approach to identifying basic functional areas remains a fundamental approach to management studies.

A later, complementary approach has been to examine the special managerial skills or techniques associated with different types of resources. Though planning, for example, is a function applicable to both personnel and buildings, managers should recognize the differences between the two. Personnel (or human resource) management, financial management, facilities management, and even records management, have developed to deal with the principal resources available to an organization.

Figure 1-1 demonstrates the complementary relationship between functional and resource management. In the resulting matrix, each resource requires appropriate managerial action across the whole range of functions. Managers with personnel responsibilities will be concerned with hiring plans, while their counterparts in finance will be more concerned with financial planning documents. Though such specialists should be permitted to focus on the areas under their control, each should be encouraged to keep in mind the overall objectives of the organization and the reciprocal and continuing effects actions in one area will have on others. (A personnel manager needs to be aware of coming financial restraints, and a money manager will take an interest in the selection of accounting personnel, for example.) This "big picture" viewpoint, while advisable at any level of management, is essential for top-level managers, even if the repository they manage is very small.

In the decades since Taylor and Fayol presented their studies, techniques and methodologies drawn from a wide range of disciplines, from the behavioral to the quantitative, have been applied to management studies. Weber's sociological perspective was succeeded in the 1920s (and beyond) by the application of psychology to management. Quantitative studies, including systems analysis and opera-

Figure 1-1 Resources and the Managerial Functions

FUNCTION:	Planning	Organizing	Staffing	Directing	Controlling
RESOURCE:					
Money	Organization's master planning (covers all resources)	multi-year financial plan	selection, training, motivation	periodic accounting data	budgets
People		hiring plan		meetings, written communication	performance review
Facilities		blueprints, building plans		repair orders	maintenance logs

tions research,[3] both developed by the RAND Corporation during the Second World War, became especially prominent in the 1950s and 1960s. Political science, with its interest in power and power relationships, assumed prominence at about the same time. The 1960s began an emphasis on such issues as participatory management.

In addition to the methodological shifts of the last eight decades, management studies have broadened far beyond their original focus on private sector, industrial organizations. Theorists like Peter Drucker have long argued that management is applicable to public and nonindustrial settings—even though the tools for measuring performance in those sectors may (for now) lack the precision of tools available for measuring corporate performance, i.e., profit. A major problem facing Drucker and others who have proclaimed the coming of the information age has been the embryonic or nonexistent states of such tools. It is one thing to tell information managers—including archivists—of the need to demonstrate to higher management that information adds value to an organization's product, and another thing altogether to calculate how much value is added. This remains one of the great challenges to contemporary management science, and one with particular bearing for the archival profession.

Organizations and Their Environments

Organizations do not exist or function in isolation. They are created to serve a purpose or set of

[3] Systems analysis, most frequently associated with electronic data systems, is the study of integrated units and functions with emphasis on the relationships between their various parts. Operations research is the application of scientific method and technique, especially quantitative analysis, to the study of organizations. The term operations research is sometimes used synonymously with "management science."

purposes, and they exist within a set of operating circumstances that will almost certainly change over time, though the pace and sources of that change will vary. Incremental change may normally occur at an unchallenging pace, but most organizations are subject to more severe transitions. A university archivist will find the pace of change accelerating if the larger university system reorganizes or adds a new department or school; likewise, a corporate archives may have to deal with the organizational consequences of a merger or takeover.

One of the key tasks facing the manager is to prepare an organization to meet its objectives and to operate in its existing environment. In the private sector, an organization's objectives and its performance within its environment (or market) are often kept in rigid alignment by financial considerations. Failure to accurately gauge the market and react appropriately to it can prove disastrous. Most archivists may feel that they are not likely to be threatened by the bankruptcy of their parent organizations, but they are not immune to environmental issues. The price of failure in the archival setting may not be bankruptcy, but it may well be a chronic shortage of resources, threatened closure, or irrelevance.

The External Environment

Organizations are not self-contained. They interact continuously with their external environment. Common elements to consider when defining an external environment include: technical factors, demographic/social factors, legal and regulatory factors, and competitive factors. An understanding of these factors and their application to the situation an organization (or profession) faces is critical to the manager's ability to prepare for future operations.

Technical Factors. Is the archives or its parent organization operating in a situation of technological stability? Will immediate or potential changes affect the technology of the product or service generated by an organization?

Clearly the technical factor most likely to alter the archival environment is the computer, which both offers new ways to control collections and confronts the profession with new types of records. The continuing development of computing technology, accompanied by the continuing decline in real computing costs, means that every archival manager will have to face the implications of the computer and all its works. What actions taken or planned by the parent organization will change the way it creates records? What steps need to be taken to enable the archives to receive and store those records?

Demographic and Social Factors. What changes in society will affect the operations of archival institutions? Though it is unlikely that any demographic change will affect the profession's operating environment as pervasively as the computer has and will, such factors cannot be ignored. For example, what impact will the aging of the U.S. population have on archives?

Figure 1-2

CHANGE	POSSIBLE EFFECTS
The aging American population	1. increased leisure time; 2. increased demand for service records; 3. increase in genealogical interest.

Are these effects good or bad for archival institutions? Do they represent problems or opportunities? In truth, they are likely to produce both. Increased use of a repository is a wonderful selling point in acquiring resources, but it also may result in increased demands on staff and added preservation problems. In this as in other areas of environmental change the manager must recognize changing conditions as early as possible, plan for them, and adjust resource allocations accordingly. This will not eliminate problems, but it should enhance an organization's ability to deal with them.

Some social and demographic factors have already had an impact on the archival profession. The changing status of women and the consequent changes in society have required any number of adaptations, ranging from the initiation of studies on women in the profession to the need to consider

child care as a fringe benefit, and to the growing demand for more flexible work schedules. Whether such changes are dramatic or evolutionary, the manager needs to take positive steps to determine when environmental change demands an institutional reaction.

Legal and Regulatory Factors. Copyright law, the contractual status of deeds and access stipulations, federal and state records acts, changes in the tax deductions for literary papers, and privacy legislation are among the more common legal issues with which archivists are familiar. Archival managers need to be aware of the laws and regulations governing their collections; they must also be cognizant of developments affecting the climate in which their institutions must operate. Changes in laws governing personnel (fair labor practices, occupational health and safety codes, equal employment opportunity, etc.), facilities (building codes, zoning, historic site preservation programs), and finance (a particularly varied set of requirements, depending on whether one manages a private, local, state, corporate, or federal archival operation) must all be considered.

Competitive Factors. At this point the reader may think that too much of the private sector mentality of management training has slipped into this manual. Archivists, after all, are not in the business of selling cars, or toothpaste, or junk bonds. They provide a valuable public service, frequently in situations where monopoly rather than competition would seem to prevail. The National Archives is, after all, *the* national archives, and it does not bid for the papers of the Foreign Agricultural Service. How many archives is the Salvation Army likely to have?

From the collection standpoint, many archives are real or virtual monopolies. Institutionally, however, even these organizations must compete for both records and resources. Archivists can find themselves in competition with organizations or individuals that do not want to surrender their records or wish to exercise their own judgment on their disposition. Manuscript repositories compete for collections. The National Archives must compete with all the other demands for money made on the federal government; the archives of the Salvation Army, indeed every archives, competes for funds. Rarely will the competitive situation for resources remain static over time. Whether that situation is improving or deteriorating, the manager's responsibility is to assess the state of the environment and the important trends developing in it and to prepare the organization to deal with them. Beyond reacting to change, the manager needs to be alert to opportunities to influence the environment in the institution's favor.

In saying that archivists "provide a valuable public service," we might have said "archivists believe they provide a valuable public service," for it is by no means certain that resource allocators and the public at large agree. Even if they agree in principle that archives are valuable, it is clear they do not agree with the profession on *how* valuable, as translated into and measured by resources. The archival manager must find a way to convince resource allocators of the repository's value, a task that requires leadership, a topic to be discussed later.

Beyond competition for records and resources, archivists may face competition for function and identity. Ask most executives to whom they would turn for advice on dealing with rare, old records, and archivists might get a reassuringly high response. Ask the same executives to whom they might turn to ensure that a new information support system can store and retrieve records over an extended period of time, and the number answering "An archivist!" might fall. Archivists (and archival managers) need to recognize that changes in information technology may be eroding the traditional divisions between the information professions. The ways in which the information professions (including librarians and archivists, as well as professionals in information systems and information resources management) adapt to their changing technical environment may determine significant changes in the size, vitality, and prestige of the professions.

The Internal Environment

Though less dramatic—and often less apparent—than external factors, internal environmental conditions affect every organization. The collective skills and experience of personnel, management styles, and established policies governing such matters as hiring, promotion, and internal communication are among the significant internal factors managers must consider. Given the length of time required to gain familiarity with large collections of documents and records, high turnover of curatorial personnel is a detriment to effective access to those collections. By the same token, an ambitious automation plan undertaken without regard for the absence of computer skills among the staff (or without a plan to remedy this deficiency) makes little sense from a managerial viewpoint.

Because archives rarely exist as independent entities, many important decisions and policies are determined outside the archives but within the parent organization. For our purposes, these factors need to be considered internal. The National Archives must, for example, hire, pay, and manage its employees in accordance with a range of laws and regulations administered by the Office of Personnel Management, among others. Whether a repository is a historical manuscripts repository or a public archives is a key question. The answer to it will say a great deal about internal environment as it pertains to access policy, acquisitions, and other functions.

Management style is itself an internal environmental factor. Is the organization entrepreneurial in its basic approach, emphasizing results and ignoring procedure? Or is it bureaucratic, with detailed procedures for virtually any action? Most archivists work in bureaucratic surroundings, and it is hard to imagine how it could be otherwise. The preservation of valuable records over long periods of time demands a continuity of procedure that makes bureaucracy of one sort or another inevitable—and even desirable. That same bureaucracy will, however, likely be less responsive to change and less supportive of innovation than will an entrepreneurial organization. Part of the manager's job is to understand the tendencies and biases of the environment in which he or she must function.

Organizational Culture

Perhaps the most nebulous aspect of an organization's environment is its culture, defined as

> a pattern of basic assumptions—invented, discovered, or developed by a given group as it learns to cope with its problems of external adaptation and internal integration— that has worked well enough to be considered valid and, therefore, to be taught to new members as the correct way to perceive, think, and feel in relation to those problems.[4]

As this definition suggests, an organization's culture is so embedded in custom and the routine of day-to-day behavior that it can be difficult to identify. In fact, a culture can become so imbedded, so natural, that occupants of the culture may find it odd that an outsider would even notice or point out some aspect

---

[4] Edgar H. Schein, *Organizational Culture and Leadership* (San Francisco: Jossey-Bass Publishers, 1985), p. 9.

of it. "Of course we do (fill in the blank) that way. How else would you do it?"

The other key to understanding cultures is to realize that they are specific. No two organizations are exactly alike, and the application of techniques and practices drawn from one institution to another can be tricky business. The hasty or thoughtless introduction of a foreign idea or practice can result in its rejection by an institution's culture. An archives will find it difficult to set itself apart from the culture of its parent organization: a state archives may have a more formal and hierarchical approach to its operations than a repository for the performing arts or a community organization. Smaller repositories, on the other hand, especially those run by the same person over a long period of time, will take on a personal "culture" that can have a rigidity of its own.

Cultures need not be static; by their very nature, it is virtually impossible for them to be completely static. Getting them to develop and change the way a manager—or even a whole management structure—wants them to can, however, be extremely difficult. In their rituals and habits, cultures can be bewildering to the outsider, and in some particulars can be easily lampooned. They nonetheless can be both useful and important, useful in the degree they provide habitual responses to recurring situations, and important in the degree to which they provide identity to a group or organization. There is nothing wrong with doing something a certain way because "we've always done it that way." This habit becomes a problem only when the circumstances in which the organization must function have changed to the point that the habitual response becomes irrelevant or harmful to the organization's ability to function.

The Managerial Role

Ezra Pound once described the poet as "the antenna of the race." Without attempting to propose management as poetry, the active manager should function as a sensor, alert to signals affecting his or her organization. Though this manual will attempt to describe tools for more effective management, perhaps its primary goal is to make the archival manager more alert to the need to apply those tools intelligently, that is, with proper regard for the unique qualities and characteristics of each institution. Compound this with the complexities of dealing with the people who make up the fundamental resource of these institutions, and the manager, even in a relatively small organization, may confront problems that will tax every intellectual, emotional, and even physical strength.

This is not an attempt to describe managers as either masochists or martyrs. The uncertainties of management, the difficulties inherent in winning support for a program or in gaining the cooperation of subordinates, peers, and higher officials, can be frustrating and even demoralizing. They can also be sources of challenge and satisfaction. For the archival manager, experience as an archival professional, with the profession's strong sense of commitment to its mission and standards, must serve as a fundamental source of energy, purpose, and persistence. The archivist turned manager should see this transformation not as the abandonment of professional skills and status, but as their extension and enhancement.

Suggested Readings

As a general reference work, it would be hard to surpass the American Management Associations, *AMA Management Handbook*. 2d ed. (New York: AMACOM, 1983). The handbook is arranged like a one-volume desk encyclopedia, with individual sections on finance, human resources management, and so on. While it contains material that may not be of use to every archival manager, it is a valuable tool nonetheless.

Henry Mintzberg, *The Nature of Managerial Work* (New York: Harper and Row, 1973) is a standard introduction to management—with emphasis on the subject of what managers actually do—and has influenced any number of subsequent works.

Joseph A. Raelin, *The Clash of Cultures* (Boston: Harvard Business School Press, 1986) and Terence E. Deal and Allen A. Kennedy, *Corporate Cultures: The Rites and Rituals of Corporate Life* (Reading, Mass.: Addison-Wesley, 1982) are extremely useful studies on the nature and problems of organizational behavior.

Edited by Lynn E. Miller, *Managing Human Service Organizations* (Westport, Conn.: Quorum Books, 1989) should be a primary reference for the professional-turned-manager.

No one has been more energetic in arguing the applicability of management techniques to the public sector than the prolific Peter Drucker. *The Age of Discontinuity* (New York: Harper and Row, 1969) and *Innovation and Entrepreneurship: Practice and Principles* (New York: Harper and Row, 1987) are both entertaining and informative.

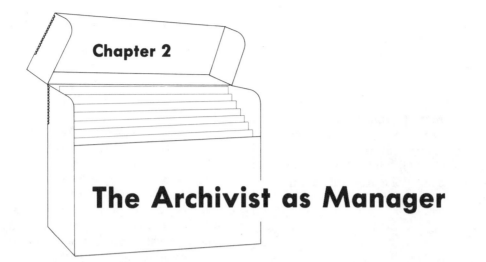

Chapter 2

The Archivist as Manager

Management focuses on the allocation of an institution's limited human, financial, and physical resources to achieve specific goals. It is a humanistic endeavor with an emphasis on relationships between resource allocators and the archival manager, the manager and peers, and the manager and subordinates. To succeed in these endeavors archival managers must succeed in managing themselves. This chapter will look at such issues as acquiring self-knowledge, leading co-workers, and establishing a vision of the archives' future.

Self-Knowledge

To be effective managers, archivists must understand themselves. As individuals, archivists must assess their personal abilities, personality traits, and the effectiveness of their interaction with superiors, peers, and subordinates. Self-understanding is problematic at best. Individual perception of one's strengths and abilities can be quite different from those of colleagues, co-workers, and friends. If individuals are to succeed as archival managers they must constantly test their perception of individual strengths and weaknesses against assessments made by others.

Individuals have specific personality traits. One may be an extrovert or an introvert, critical or supportive, sympathetic or indifferent. By developing a knowledge of one's strengths and weaknesses, the archival administrator can better relate to others. An introvert may take a public speaking course to encourage confidence, while someone who feels they are overly critical may make a strong ef-

fort to develop a more positive, supportive demeanor when dealing with staff members. Without making an effort to know oneself, such steps cannot be taken. An understanding of personal traits allows the archival administrator to carry out tasks more successfully. For example, an administrator who is not detail oriented may seek assistants with such skills to balance the management team. Archival administrators must continually evaluate their personal abilities and use such knowledge in the selection and promotion of other staff members.

Archivists must also develop an understanding of their professional skills and career goals. What is most important in a job—administering an interesting collection or solving an unusual set of administrative tasks? Is recognition by professional peers important? What types of archival tasks are the most interesting? Which tasks bring the greatest success? Is being a midlevel administrator in a large repository more satisfying than having full administrative responsibility in a small archives? Is one's strength in technical areas, such as arrangement and description, or in dealing with people in reference or archival acquisition? Is the individual detail oriented or more concerned with the larger picture?

Archival administrators must also be aware of their personal managerial style. Do they tend to be more collegial or authoritarian in their approach? What type of management style is prevalent within the parent institution? Management style can be an important issue, and clashes between individuals with an authoritarian style in a collegial environment and a collegial style in an authoritarian institution are not uncommon. Avoiding such problems requires archival administrators either to be flexible in their approach or seek employment in an institution with a comparable management style.

Self-knowledge is a continuing search, and there are never simple answers or solutions. Archival managers will have more personal satisfaction and achieve greater success if they develop an understanding of their personal and professional motivation. Such an understanding will allow decisions to be based on real needs and assist the archival administrator in making choices based on reason rather than intuition.

Leadership

Leadership is a personal trait, often defined as charisma, authoritative decision making, power to influence other people's opinions, or ability to inspire a supportive and loyal following. Not all individuals are singled out as leaders, but nearly everyone has some leadership skills. For some, leadership is expressed in the work place, while others display it in clubs, churches, or voluntary activities. It is also true that not all persons in authority necessarily have leadership skills. Many positions in a bureaucracy receive their power or authority from their rank rather than from the individual's particular skills as a leader. Such legitimized authority is given to department heads, church bishops, or publicly elected officials. That such individuals have power does not necessary ensure that they can lead, and their failure often contributes to stagnation or institutional collapse. As managers, archivists have such legitimized authority. To use this power to lead, however, managers must develop leadership skills which take them beyond the authority to make decisions. (See Figure 2-1.)

Vision

One of the most important components of leadership is vision. It is the ability to imagine the results of both individual and group efforts. Skilled archival administrators envision what their repositories will achieve in one, five, and ten years. While the road map to this achievement is an archival plan, the image exists before the plan is drafted. Like plans, visions are not static. A vision can be affected by outside factors and must reflect current realities. Vision is affected by an archival administrator's breadth and depth of both experience and training. Archivists who have seen a wide variety of arrangement techniques or reference situations are better

Figure 2-1   Archival Leadership Skills

1. Leaders develop the team concept, choosing people with varying talents and allowing them to do what they do best, while simultaneously moving them toward an assigned goal.
2. Leaders think of renewal, developing strong values, new skills, and new leaders within the staff.
3. Leaders have good motivation skills and encourage their subordinates.
4. Leaders have good political skills and are able to resolve or reconcile conflicts and satisfy constituencies both inside and outside the repository.
5. Leaders seek to influence people outside the archives. They communicate not only the archives' intrinsic importance and purpose, but also its value to the larger organization.
6. Leaders see difficult situations not as problems, but as opportunities for seeking solutions.
7. Leaders are calm in the face of adversity. When faced with a challenge, they look for solutions rather than scapegoats.

able to envision how they will carry out these tasks than someone who is inexperienced or who has experience in only one repository. Persons with vision have a broad perception of their role in the archives, the role of the repository within its parent institution, and the role of the institution in society. (See Figure 2-2.)

Using Leadership and Vision to Achieve Goals

Archival managers are responsible for mobilizing the resources of the repository, the parent organization, and outside sources to achieve specific goals. To accomplish this, archivists must use leadership skills to influence a variety of groups and individuals both within and outside the repository.

Archival managers must begin by believing in themselves and the goals they set for their institutions. Too many archivists in small repositories either do not have specific goals or do not believe strongly enough in them to fight, argue, or cajole others into supporting the archival program. Managers in larger institutions must influence the archival staff, getting members to agree on goals and plans

Figure 2-2   Vision

1. Leaders develop a vision of what they want to achieve as individuals.
2. Leaders develop a clear understanding of the parent institution, an appreciation of the role the repository plays within the institution, and a vision of what the archives should achieve.
3. Leaders have a vision of the goals of the profession and can adjust their institutional vision to support and enhance those goals.
4. Leaders have a clear understanding of the parent institution's history and culture and are able to assist their parent institution in developing a vision of the future based upon past achievements.
5. Having a vision of the future, archival leaders have the ability to select courses of action which will lead to those goals, rejecting or delaying tasks which can be done at some future date.

and devising work plans to achieve them. Whether working in a single-person archives or one with many staff members, the manager must believe in the cause and lead others to believe as well.

To be successful, the archival manager must identify the individuals critical to success and seek their support for the archives' goals. These persons include: the leaders of the parent institution, immediate superiors, peers in other departments, subordinates, donors, researchers, and the general public. Each group looks at the repository from a different perspective, and the archival leader must use different methods to gain their support.

After identifying those constituencies critical to the success of the program, managers must define strategies to gain support for the goals. Archivists can assess the perceptions and motivations of different constituencies, appealing for their support and developing a stronger following for the archives. Only when a manager combines leadership skills, a strong will to achieve, and the ability to clearly define goals, will real archival progress be made.

There are many reasons why people support a particular program or person. Some of these include:

1. A record of success. If an individual or institution has been successful in achieving substantive goals or concrete re-

sults, people will be more likely to give their support. Has the manuscripts repository acquired significant collections which have brought prestige or fame to the parent institution? Does the repository have a reputation of meeting the deadlines of the parent institution's administrators and staff?

2. A belief in expertise. Specialists such as archivists can gain support because of their perceived special abilities or knowledge. Such support can be enhanced by a strong professional reputation or visible achievements in professional organizations.

3. A belief in the repository's mission. Persons who have been closely involved with the repository as donors or researchers will have a better understanding of its role in preservation and research and are more likely to support its program.

The support of a variety of constituencies is critical to the archives' success in achieving its goals. However, without the leadership and vision of the archival manager, these groups cannot be organized and directed toward a common purpose.

Time Management

Time is perhaps the most important resource archivists possess. Archives are labor-intensive; they do not require the latest high-technology equipment, expensive laboratories, or design studios. Their primary needs are space and time: time to identify and acquire, time to process, time to conserve, and time to provide reference services.

In carrying out managerial tasks, archivists must ensure that their time and their employees' time is used to achieve the repository's goals. Archivists, faced with an overwhelming number of tasks and only a finite amount of time to complete them, can only accomplish them by:

1. Spending more time at work,
2. Doing work more quickly or efficiently,
3. Delegating work to others, including para-professional staff,
4. Eliminating tasks which do not lead to the achievement of archival goals.

To spend time more wisely, archivists must organize themselves for the day, the week, the month, and the year by establishing both institutional and personal goals. After such goals have been set, archi-

Figure 2-3   Time Log

Priority Rating			
1 important and urgent	2 important, not urgent	3 routine	4 not business related

MONDAY, JUNE 1

Time	Activity	Duration	Priority	Comments
8 am	Long-range plan	15 minutes	1	
8:15	Phone call	15 minutes	2	Boss calling to discuss employee annual review.
8:30	Long-range plan	30 minutes	1	
9:00	Staff meeting	75 minutes	3	Meeting dragged on too long, people wouldn't stick to the agenda. Reference archivist wanted to discuss personnel issues which were inappropriate.
10:15	Coffee	15 minutes	3	
10:30	Meeting with mobile shelving representative	30 minutes	2	Discussed shelving specifications for new addition.
11:00	Long-range plan	10 minutes	1	
11:10	Husband called	15 minutes	4	
11:25	Colleague called	40 minutes	3	Called about a reference for a former employee.
12:05	Lunch	40 minutes	3	

vists must evaluate how their time is spent and whether it is actively used to achieve goals.

Completing a time log is one of the most common ways managers evaluate their use of time. Such logs record the time of day, the type of activity, and its duration, and allow managers to rate that activity in relation to personal and institutional goals. To evaluate the use of time, the archival manager should complete a time log on a periodic basis. Such a time log should be kept over three to ten workdays, preferably during a period when the archivist is carrying out normal duties. When the log is complete, the archivist must evaluate how the time was spent. Did the activities lead toward personal or institutional goals? Was time wasted on activities which could have been done by someone else or not done at all? Such an evaluation will assist the archivist in revising patterns of behavior which are not goal-oriented so that time can be used to maximum advantage. (See Figure 2-3.)

Making the best use of personal time also implies self-understanding. The archivist should rank tasks in order of importance, attending to the highest priority tasks first. If writing is an important aspect of one's work, it should be scheduled at a time of greatest effectiveness. For many, this is early in the morning, while others can write on late into the night. Individuals must evaluate their own personality and working situation so that time is used effec-

tively to achieve both personal and institutional goals.

Effective Communication

An archival manager must communicate effectively and efficiently with each constituency. In addition to reviewing the use of personal time, archival managers must develop patterns of communication and work that increase their efficiency. Communication can range from a memorandum to a newsletter and from brief one-on-one discussions to large staff meetings lasting hours. Archival managers should always choose the means of communication which achieves their goal with the least amount of effort.

Meetings are one of the most time-consuming activities of institutional life and can either waste or save time, depending on how they are organized. Poorly organized meetings that do not lead toward archival goals should never be called since they consume not only the archival manager's time, but also the time of everyone else who attends the meeting. The archival manager should consider other alternatives before calling a meeting. Providing information or issuing a report can be done by letter or written memorandum. A meeting should be called only when there is a need for two-way conversation among those invited.

Figure 2-4   Meeting Agenda

> **NEW CHURCH ARCHIVES**
> **Staff Meeting Agenda**
>
> Tuesday, April 7, 1990
> 9:00–10:00 A.M.
>
> A. Old Business
>   1. March statistical report—Director
>   2. Report on the new facility plans—Assistant Director
>   3. Discussion of changes in the Saturday morning staff roster—Reference Archivist
> B. New Business
>   1. Proposal to develop a repository disaster plan—Preservation Officer
>   2. Report on changes in the New Church Archives personnel code—Director
> C. Next Meeting Date

If a meeting is required, it should be kept short and to the point. A written agenda should always be prepared and sent to persons attending the meeting. The chair must hold the meeting to the agenda items and not let the discussion stray to other issues and topics. The chair should always start the meeting on time, not waiting for stragglers to join the group. Before the meeting starts, a time limit for the meeting and for agenda items should be established. A time limit forces those attending the meeting to get through the agenda in an expeditious manner. If the chair has miscalculated the amount of time needed to complete the meeting, another meeting can be scheduled for a later date. Too often, meetings expand from the time needed to complete a task to the time available. Setting a time limit alleviates this problem.

Organizing Paperwork

Archival managers must organize the paperwork which flows across the desk if they wish to use their time most efficiently. This requires a well-organized filing system so that material is filed and retrieved in an expeditious manner. In addition to subject files, the archivist should have a bring-up or "tickler" system where letters requiring a follow-up response are filed. Arranged on a monthly basis for the upcoming twelve months, it can be subdivided by days for the current month. Such a system will ensure adequate follow-up to acquisition requests or other letters where a response is awaited.

Many archivists have responsibility for records management within their parent institutions. In developing record retention schedules and procedures, the archives' own records should not be overlooked. Inactive records should be regularly removed from active files. Scheduled records should be retired as soon as the retention date has been reached, and archival managers should also apply other records management techniques such as forms and files management to their own records.

Archival managers can reduce the volume of correspondence by using the telephone, by delegating the work, or by using personalized form letters. Computer word-processing is especially helpful in composing form paragraphs for a variety of letters and can save considerable time in acknowledging donations or answering reference questions. Newer technologies such as the fax machine and electronic mail by computer network are other methods which archival managers should investigate to speed and simplify their communications.

Other Time-Savers

Archival managers must make every effort to conserve their time. One method is careful evaluation of voluntary tasks, such as professional responsibilities, internal working groups, or task forces. Although such tasks are sometimes required, archival administrators often have a choice of whether or not to assume responsibility for a specific job. When that is the case, the archival administrator should carefully evaluate whether assuming responsibility will assist or hinder personal or institutional goals and make an appropriate decision. In addition to reviewing whether or not a task supports institutional or personal goals, archival administrators must also ensure that they do not take on more tasks than it is possible to complete. Not only is such action irresponsible, but there is every likelihood that the tasks will be done poorly, if at all.

Using the telephone can also save time. A telephone call is quicker than a letter, and a conference call can save both travel costs and travel time if it replaces a face-to-face meeting. It is almost always less expensive to use the telephone than to write a letter when staff time for typing and filing and storage costs are considered. The telephone certainly has many advantages, but it can also be a source of wasted time if used improperly. In a multiperson office, a secretary should screen all incoming calls providing needed assistance to the caller or referring the call appropriately. In a small repository, an answering machine can be used to reduce interruptions when dealing with researchers or important projects. The archival manager can also be more effective by organizing telephone time. Calls should be grouped together at the beginning or the end of the day to avoid interrupting other work. When making calls, the archivist should know what issues need discussion or clarification and avoid idle discussion whenever possible.

Conclusion

The success or failure of archival programs is often very closely linked to an individual archival manager. Certainly many achievements are the result of a group effort and reflect the participation of many individuals. Nonetheless, moving the group to achieve is the archival manager's responsibility and reflects individual success or failure. However, indi-

vidual leadership and vision are not enough. For long-term success, the archival manager must develop an organizational structure which provides an institutional base for achieving archival goals.

Suggested Readings

Good introductory books include: Merrill E. Douglas et. al., *Manage Your Time, Manage Your Work, Manage Yourself* (New York: American Management Associations, 1985); Donald H. Weiss, *How to Be a Successful Manager* (New York: American Management Associations, 1986); Donald L. Kirkpatrick, *How to Plan and Conduct Productive Business Meetings* (New York: American Management Associations, 1986); and D. H. Weiss, *Get Organized! How to Control Your Life through Self-Management* (New York: American Management Associations, 1986).

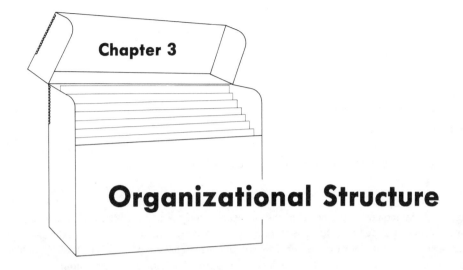

Chapter 3

Organizational Structure

Organizational structure reflects both internal and external institutional relationships and policies such as the archives' placement within its parent organization, its internal hierarchy, and its relationship with auxiliary structures such as advisory boards. These topics may seem relevant only for larger repositories or those which have been established for a long time. Nothing could be further from the truth. All archives have a structure, whether it is described in writing, whether the archives is administered by a "lone arranger," or whether it has a staff of two hundred. Developing an organizational structure is a fundamental responsibility of every archival administrator. For a repository to operate effectively, it must formalize its structure. Policies, organizational structures, and reporting relationships cannot be left to the whim of the current archivist or superiors. The absence of a formal structure will cause confusion among staff, researchers, and donors, and may well lead to major failures in the archival system. (See Figure 3-1.)

Authority and Purpose

Since they are responsible for preserving the records of their parent institutions, all archives are part of larger structures. Manuscript repositories may be independent in theory, but most are part of libraries or historical societies. As part of a larger agency, a repository has a specific mission, responsibility, and authority. If the archives is a governmental agency, its functions are usually dictated by government statute or regulation. Corporate and religious archives often have their activities outlined in bylaws, constitutions, or institutional policies. A university archives may have its activities governed or directed by the board of trustees or by the action of its president or provost.

Whatever the type of repository, it is the responsibility of the archival administrator to develop a formal statement which outlines its mission, responsibility, and authority in relation to its parent institution. Such a statement should reflect the ability and authority of the archives to collect and preserve records. It should specify the provisions which enable the staff to carry out such tasks. The statement should address the issue of the disposition of archival records in the event the archives or the parent institution should no longer exist. Finally, the statement should delineate the system of accountability for any specialized programs such as

Figure 3-1

Overview of Organizational Structure
A. Relationship with the Parent Institution
1. Authority and purpose
2. Organizational placement
3. Governing board
4. Informal networks
B. Auxiliary Structures
1. Archives advisory committee
2. Friends of the archives
C. Internal Organization
1. Organizational chart
2. Policies and procedures

Figure 3-2

Policy Statement

1. Value of a Policy Statement
  A. Creates a public statement of archival purpose.

  B. Defines a collecting policy.

  C. Defines an access policy.

  D. Outlines the parameters of the archivist's responsibility and authority.

2. Outlines of a Policy Statement
  A. Legal authority

   The statement must begin by indicating the name of the repository and the name of the parent institution; it should outline the archives' legal authority to collect, preserve, and make available its records. Such a statement should prohibit the removal of material from the archives without the archivist's approval as well as outline what should happen to the collection in the event that the archival program is dissolved or disbanded.

  B. Purpose

   The archives must have a mission statement defining archival duties and tasks.(See Chapter 4 on planning.)

  C. Position and authority of the archivist

   The statement should outline the archivist's role within the archives as well as the relationship with the parent institution or governing board. It should detail the archivist's legal authority to carry out archival tasks and may indicate general qualifications for the archivist and a method of selecting appropriate personnel.

  D. Outline of responsibilities

   The policy statement should outline specific duties for the archivist and archival staff. This should indicate appropriate relationships between the archives and the parent institution, the archives and an advisory committee (if one exists), the archives and donors, and the archives and researchers.

  E. Collecting policy

   This should indicate why the archives exists and what type of material is collected. (This may be supplemented by a separate and more detailed collecting policy.)

  F. Access policy

   There should be a general statement outlining who may use the archives collection and under what conditions. (This may be supplemented by a separate and more detailed access policy.)

  G. Records management

   If the archives is responsible for records management, this role should be carefully delineated.

  H. Definitions

   The statement should clarify archival responsibility by defining such archival terms as archives, records, access, and appraisal in the policy statement.

Concept courtesy Society of California Archivists

---

records management. (See Figure 3-2.) This policy document must be authorized by the institution's highest administrative body. Such authority allows archivists to carry out their responsibility without questions being raised about the support of the parent agency.

Organizational Placement

One of the important issues for any repository is its placement in the institution's organizational structure. The archives' position in the larger organizational structure can either enhance or hinder it in carrying out its mission. In addition, the archival administrator must have a clear understanding of the lines of communication and authority and be able to develop strong and supportive working relationships with superiors.

The repository's placement will vary depending upon the type of parent institution and its mission.

Placement can have a major impact on an archives' program, impinging on such issues as:

1. The ability of the archives to carry out its mission.
2. The level of financial and program support for the archives.
3. The commonality of purpose between the archives and the department which supervises its activities.

There is no one perfect solution, and placements vary even among comparable types of institutions. (See Figures 3-3 and 3-4.)

Given a choice, what type of placement should an archivist seek? First, an archivist should attempt to locate the repository as close to the top of the

Figure 3-3

Typical Examples of Archival Placement

State Archives: Secretary of State, State Library, Department of Administrative Services, State Historical Society.

University Archives: University President or Provost, Library, Public Relations, University Secretary or Registrar.

Institutional or Corporate Archives: Corporate Secretary, Public Relations, Library, Legal Affairs, Management Information Systems.

Figure 3-4

A comparison of the positive and negative aspects of placing a university archives under the university library as opposed to the president's office.

President's Office

Positive features:

1. The president's office has authority over the entire university campus and can mandate the transfer of records or the development of records retention schedules.
2. The president has greater discretion in budgeting funds and staff needed to carry out an archival program.

Negative features:

1. The president's office seldom deals with either information management or the tools needed to carry out such functions.
2. The training and institutional outlook of the president's staff is dissimilar to those of the archives' staff. While understanding the administrative value of preserving records, the president's staff may fail to see the importance of making material available; they may even oppose access by researchers.

University Library

Positive features:

1. Both archives and libraries deal with information packaged in various forms.
2. Libraries have bibliographic networks which may be used by the archives to describe its collection.
3. Librarians and archivists usually have similar training and are committed to making materials available for use.

Negative features:

1. In a library setting, an archives may be several administrative levels from the top library official, who is in turn several levels below the rank of the senior university administrator. Such distance can make it difficult to obtain support and cooperation for a university-wide archival program.
2. An archives is one function within a library and may fail to receive an adequate budget or support staff.
3. Because library administrators may not understand archives, they may not support a strong, separate archival program.

administrative hierarchy as possible. Archivists are generally able to generate much greater support and cooperation if they report to the library director rather than to the assistant head of the department of special collections. Second, the archives should establish a separate identity. Whenever possible, it should have a separate budget line, annual report, or any other tool which will allow greater independence and institutional stature. Third, the archives should seek placement under a department with a strong interest in archives that can give it adequate support. Fourth, the archives should seek placement in a department which has a successful record of accomplishment.

Although archivists in an established program may not have the optimum placement in the institutional hierarchy, change is sometimes possible. A move to a different department is probably easiest soon after a repository is established. When no long-term administrative or personal relationship has been established, an archives can be moved from one department to another with no negative repercussions. The archivist may not be able to instigate such a change, but it can sometimes be done by a strong supporter within the institutional structure.

Another appropriate time for change often occurs during a major reorganization of the parent institution, such as a time of internal restructuring resulting from a corporate takeover or the merging of a number of functions within an organization. If the repository is dissatisfied with its institutional placement, changing it is more feasible during institutional change. Again, this will require cultivating supporters who can assist the archives in making this change as well as finding a department willing to accept responsibility for the archives program.

A final method of bringing about change in institutional placement is through an overall review of the archival program by appointing an archival consultant, convening a "blue-ribbon" citizens' committee, or undertaking an institutional self-study program. As outside observers, either consultants or a citizens' committee can be a strong force for change. As disinterested parties, their advice is more readily acceptable and may be followed more closely than information received directly from those involved in the archival program. The only danger to the repository is the possibility that the recommendations may not be what the archives hoped for when it requested or accepted such a review. An institutional self-study keeps decision making under the archives' control and might indicate whether there is a need for an outside review.

The placement of the repository within its parent organization is the basic foundation for all archival programs. The ability of an archives to achieve its goals is directly related to the resources which are provided by the institution, and placement can be all-important in gaining needed resources. Strong support will not always lead to an outstanding archival program if the administrator is a poor leader, but the lack of support will inevitably lead to failure, even under the best archival administrator.

Formal Reporting Structures

Wherever the repository is located, the archivist must develop a good working relationship with those who have administrative responsibility for the archives program, whether it is one individual or a governing board. A governing board, in contrast to an advisory committee, usually has authority to approve or disapprove policies and procedures recommended by the archival administrator. Their decisions may be final, or they may be only an intermediary with their recommendations needing the approval of some higher authority. In a few cases the governing board may have actual responsibility for the overall archival program, with the unfortunate result that the archivist has no vote or direct involvement in decision making.

In any case, it must be clear to whom the archival administrator reports. Receiving direction from more than one source may lead to disruption and confusion. Such situations arise if the parent institution's chain of command is poorly defined, or if different members of a governing body express different goals for the repository and attempt to impose them. In such cases, archival administrators must define such relationships so it is clear to whom the archives reports.

Good communication is one of the most important factors in formal structures. The archival administrator must make a continual effort to inform the governing authority of all major aspects of the archival program. Such communication can take a number of forms. One is the periodic written report, whether weekly, monthly, or quarterly. A written report should describe the full range of archival activities, highlighting achievements and indicating problems that have arisen since the previous report. It can be supplemented by an informal commentary by the archival administrator when the report is presented. At the end of each year, a formal written report should be presented to the governing authority relating goals to achievements and including a detailed statistical analysis of different archival functions.

A second reporting relationship involves the development and expenditure of the archives' budget. Such negotiations begin with an initial discussion between the archival administrator and the governing body indicating the general parameters of the budget, giving a maximum budget figure or percentage increase, or laying out other standards. When the budget is complete, it is presented to the governing body for approval and, if necessary, passed further up the governing structure of the parent organization for ultimate approval. During the course of the financial year there may be a need for further discussion on budget issues if the parent organization requires budget cuts or the repository finds some unforseen needs which require an expenditure beyond the amount which is budgeted. (See Chapter 6 for further information on budgets.)

Informal Networks

Both placement and reporting structures are important, but the archives can also seek support through the informal networks which exist in every organization. Archival administrators should seek out and cultivate other departmental administrators in the larger parent organization.

One purpose in developing such informal networks is to educate other parts of the organization about the value of archives and to bolster support for the archival program. This can be accomplished by providing good archival service, by discussing the organization's concerns informally at meetings, coffee breaks, or lunch, by offering assistance to other departments with program ideas, or by serving on committees and task forces which affect other parts of the parent organization. Through positive interaction with other departments, the repository can gain influence and publicize the significance of its work. Other department administrators may not control the archives' resources, but they can support it in committees and in the informal discussion which occurs within every organization.

An informal network can also prove useful in the allocation and use of common resources. After developing good working relationships with other department heads, the archival administrator can often call upon them for support in archival projects. Examples of such support might include help from the public relations department in developing a brochure, the donation of staff time from the finance department to explain the uses of noncurrent financial records, or the assistance of the microfilm department in copying records.

Such assistance cannot be gained without considerable effort on the part of the archival administrator and the archives staff. Informal networking requires time and a fair amount of give and take. To be successful, the repository must be willing to provide services to other departments which may go beyond normal reference services. If the archives observes a need in another department which it can fill, the archives should tactfully offer a solution. Taking such initiatives will develop a reserve of good will which can be called upon later.

An informal network is important to ensure that the repository receives timely information, often outside normal channels. Communication is an ever-increasing problem within modern organizations. While there has been an increase in communications technology such as the telephone, xerox machine, computer, and the fax machine, getting the right information to the right person at the right time remains a challenge. Part of the difficulty lies in the very structure which the organization creates. By establishing an organizational chart and using this structure as the only basis for communication, departments that should receive certain information often don't, while those that do not need the information often do. An informal network is valuable because it supplements the formal lines of communication. Archivists who develop close relationships with other department heads and employees may receive valuable information which they might not receive otherwise. It is common to learn of an institutional project where the archives could participate or provide useful services, only to learn that it is too late to offer assistance. In some cases, informal communication can provide timely information, and archival administrators and their staffs should develop informal networks to achieve this end.

Archives Advisory Committee

Both formal structures and informal networks can assist the administrator in achieving institutional goals. Support organizations can serve as both buffers and advocates for the archives' cause. One such organization is the advisory committee, normally established to advise the archival administrator. Such committees, usually appointed by the parent organization, can be drawn from the institutional hierarchy, the research community, or influential donors. Depending upon the type of institution, the advisory committee has the potential to serve the repository both as an advocate and as a communication network, bringing information to the archival administrator and disseminating information to other members of the parent body. Advisory committees should provide advice and communication if they are to have any value. If an advisory committee's authority goes beyond advice and communication, its authority should be clearly delineated so that it is clear to whom the archivist reports.

Establishing an advisory committee can be particularly beneficial for a new archival program where new policies and procedures must be established. Where the archivist has recently joined a new institution, an advisory committee can be particularly helpful by serving as a sounding board, providing insights into the corporate culture, or providing a ready-made communication network.

If members are carefully selected, the committee can represent a variety of constituencies important to the repository. They can speak for the archives to resource allocators, provide specialized knowledge and expertise, and serve as informal publicists for the archives' cause. The archival administrator should carefully review not only how committee members are appointed, but who is appointed. Ideally archivists have ultimate control over who is appointed. Archivists should carefully evaluate the names put forward for an advisory committee, however, whether or not they have ultimate control over the final appointment.

The archival administrator must ensure that the advisory committee meets the needs of the repository, and that its role does not exceed its authority. To remain effective, archival administrators must maintain control of all internal archival policies and procedures, since only they have the professional training and experience to make these decisions. In most cases the balance between advice and control by an archives advisory committee can be easily maintained, but care must be used if the archives is to remain independent and carry out its professional responsibilities.

Friends of the Archives

If the repository seeks publicity and financial support rather than communication and advice, the archival administrator might consider starting a Friends of the Archives Committee. A friends group has a narrower responsibility, focusing primarily on financial support and outreach. A group of friends or benefactors is a voluntary association. It generally

Dr. Edwin C. Bridges (left), director of the Alabama Department of Archives and History, at a reception following a meeting of the Friends of the Archives. (*Barbara B. Taylor, courtesy Department of Archives and History, State of Alabama*)

operates under a constitution and bylaws with an elected board and officers.

A friends group expands the number of people actively involved in the work and support of the repository. It is usually made up of donors, researchers, and interested supporters and can be a useful support organization, while not interfering with the archival administrator's ability to control the archives' internal operation. It can serve as a pool of volunteers to work part-time as docents or indexers, provide introductions to sources of outside funding, host receptions for archival exhibits, support scholarly programs, print publications, or reproduce important documents for sale or gifts. It can also provide useful sources of information and personal introductions for collection development.

Internal Organizational Structure

Developing a structure for internal archival relationships, especially in a new archival program

**NEW YORK STATE ARCHIVES AND RECORDS ADMINISTRATION
JUNE 1990**

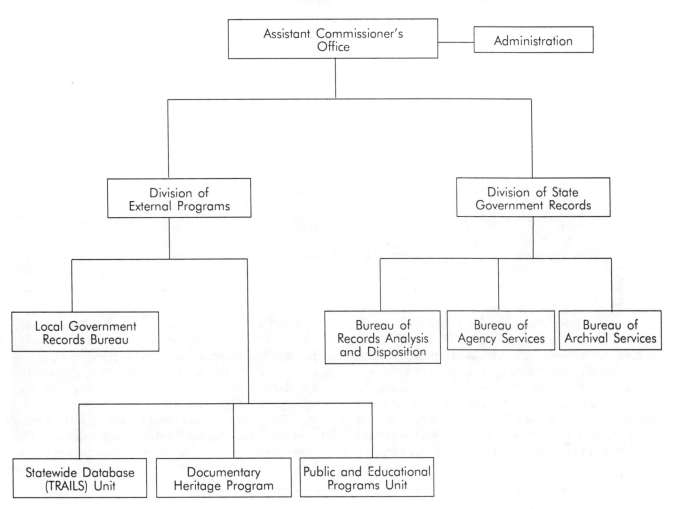

Organizational chart of a large state archival and records administration unit. (*New York State Archives and Records Administration*)

where such relationships do not already exist, is one of the most important tasks of an archival administrator. Internal organization is also of great concern in an established program, since there is a tendency for relationships to evolve over time, without an established pattern or written documentation.

A well-organized and well-defined internal structure is extremely important for any successful archival program. Such a structure defines individual and departmental responsibilities. If carefully planned, it helps the archives operate without overlapping activities and helps to ensure that all employees are aware of their tasks and responsibilities. An internal structure is defined through decisions made by the archival administrator and the staff, but these decisions are formalized and written as organizational charts, job descriptions, flow charts, and archival policies and procedures manuals.

What is an organizational chart? It is a pictorial representation of the overall structure of an archival institution. All the functional parts of the archives are included in the chart. In addition, the parts are linked by lines which show the formal paths of communication, and the departments arranged in a hierarchical fashion indicating who is responsible for supervision and direction. An organizational chart defines reporting and communication relationships within an institution. While such a document may not seem essential for a small archives, it is a useful tool to document lines of communication. While optional for smaller archives, an organizational chart is a necessity in a large archival setting.

Flow Charts

An organizational chart can be very useful but it is only a skeletal outline. It shows basic relation-

Figure 3-5   Typical Institutional Archives Organizational Chart

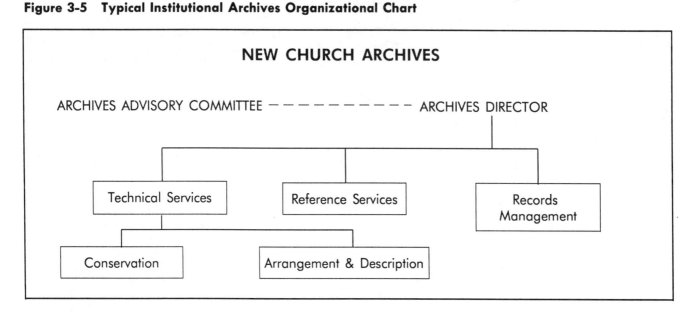

ships between departments, but it does not show in detail their interaction or responsibilities. Such activities are more commonly shown through flow charts which indicate how work and activities are carried out. For example, flow charts can show the various steps which must be taken in acquiring, processing, conserving, and providing reference service for collections acquired by the repository. While each of these four major functions are the primary respon-

sibility of different departments, tasks often overlap, are carried on simultaneously, or are affected by another department's actions. A flow chart is designed to identify each department's responsibility and clarify ambiguities in a written and pictorial fashion. (See Figure 3-7.)

Both organizational and flow charts are means of establishing organizational relationships for the archives itself or its constituent departments. Below

Figure 3-6   Typical University Archives Organizational Chart

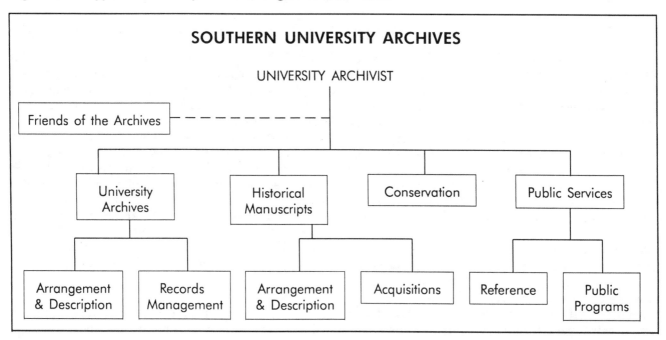

this level are the working relationships between individual archivists and between archivists and their supervisors.

Policies and Procedures

Archival administrators must establish employee responsibilities. Job descriptions provide a general outline of the tasks for which each employee is responsible. However, these tasks must be refined and standardized if the repository is to carry out its responsibilities in a consistent manner. Consistency is developed by establishing policies and procedures.

A policy is a governing principle which provides overall guidance to the way in which an archives conducts its business. A repository should, in the course of its development, establish a wide range of policies. Some of the more common include: access, personnel, collection development, deaccessioning, and copying. Each policy statement provides overall guidance to staff members. For example, an access policy may indicate who may use archival collections, when they are open for research, and how researchers can gain access to closed collections. However, this guidance is only general in nature, and is refined and standardized through the use of specific archival procedures.

Procedures dictate particular courses of action and are frequently codified through written manuals. An access policy outlines who may use archival collections and under what circumstances, but procedures outline how staff members are to deal with researchers when they visit or write to the archives. For example, access procedures would cover such issues as where the personal belongings of researchers are to be placed, whether researchers must sign a daily register or reader's form, how archival request slips are to be used, and what specific steps should be taken when a researcher asks for a restricted collection.

Archival administrators can ensure that all employees carry out their duties in a similar manner if they develop standardized procedures. Written manuals can greatly assist the training of new staff members. They also serve as a point of reference when questions arise about how staff members should proceed when dealing with an unfamiliar question or problem.

When policies and procedures are created, there should be a period set aside to instruct staff members on their use. Such a program may be formal or informal in nature, depending upon the size of the repository. An instruction period allows staff members to react to changes in the archives' operation, and staff input may modify and improve the procedures that have been suggested. Employees who are not adequately instructed in an institution's policies and procedures may misinterpret them. Inadvertently, their actions may contradict the repository's governing policies. (See Chapter 5, Human Resources, for more information on both job descriptions and staff training.)

Communication

All repositories must develop standardized policies, procedures, and job descriptions, but these must be supplemented by detailed and continuing communication among all staff members. Every archives should develop a means of structured communication among its staff.

The most common means of communication is a staff meeting. In a smaller repository staff meetings may not be scheduled regularly, but might be called only to discuss specific issues or concerns. In a larger archives where staff members see each other less frequently, staff meetings should be scheduled on a regular basis. Whether scheduled regularly or infrequently, all staff meetings should have a purpose and a structure. Not only a means of communicating information from top to bottom, staff meetings should be a forum for open discussion. Open communication allows interests, problems, and concerns to surface, allowing for solutions before problems occur.

Formal meetings can greatly assist internal communication among staff members, but informal meetings will remain the primary avenue of communication between archival administrators, supervisors, and staff members. Problems and concerns surface on a daily basis, and it is the responsibility of archival administrators to be available to listen, offer advice, and suggest solutions. Informal communication occurs naturally and easily if archival administrators are available and accessible. There should be a continuing effort to talk to staff members at their desks and worktables, to discover what they are doing, and to seek out problems and concerns. Employees respond to genuine and enthusiastic interest. If the administrator or supervisor is open and develops a pleasant working relationship with staff members, such concerns will come up naturally. The development of such informal communication cannot be overlooked and is an extremely important factor in the success of an archival program.

Figure 3-7

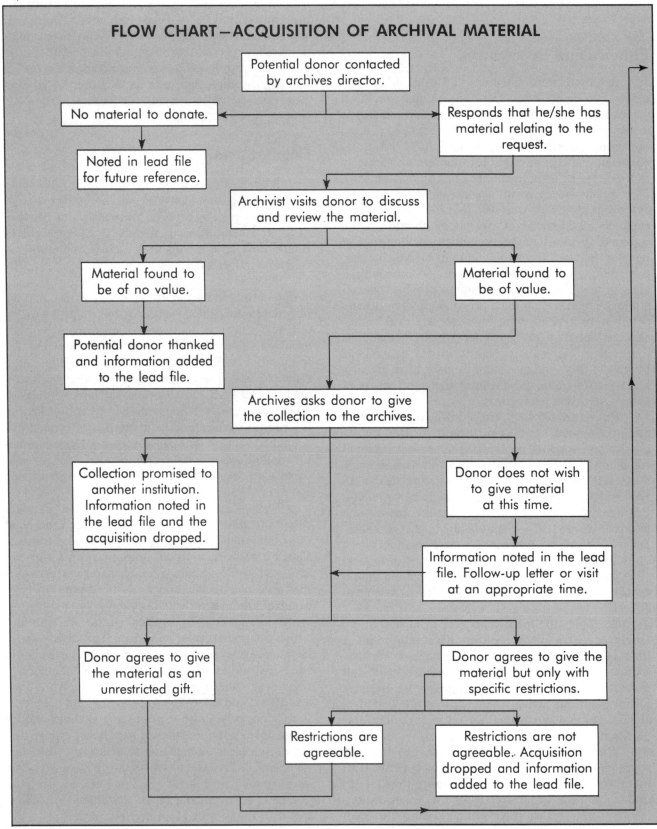

FLOW CHART—ACQUISITION OF ARCHIVAL MATERIAL

Potential donor contacted by archives director.

No material to donate.

Responds that he/she has material relating to the request.

Noted in lead file for future reference.

Archivist visits donor to discuss and review the material.

Material found to be of no value.

Material found to be of value.

Potential donor thanked and information added to the lead file.

Archives asks donor to give the collection to the archives.

Collection promised to another institution. Information noted in the lead file and the acquisition dropped.

Donor does not wish to give material at this time.

Information noted in the lead file. Follow-up letter or visit at an appropriate time.

Donor agrees to give the material as an unrestricted gift.

Donor agrees to give the material but only with specific restrictions.

Restrictions are agreeable.

Restrictions are not agreeable. Acquisition dropped and information added to the lead file.

Figure 3-7 Continued

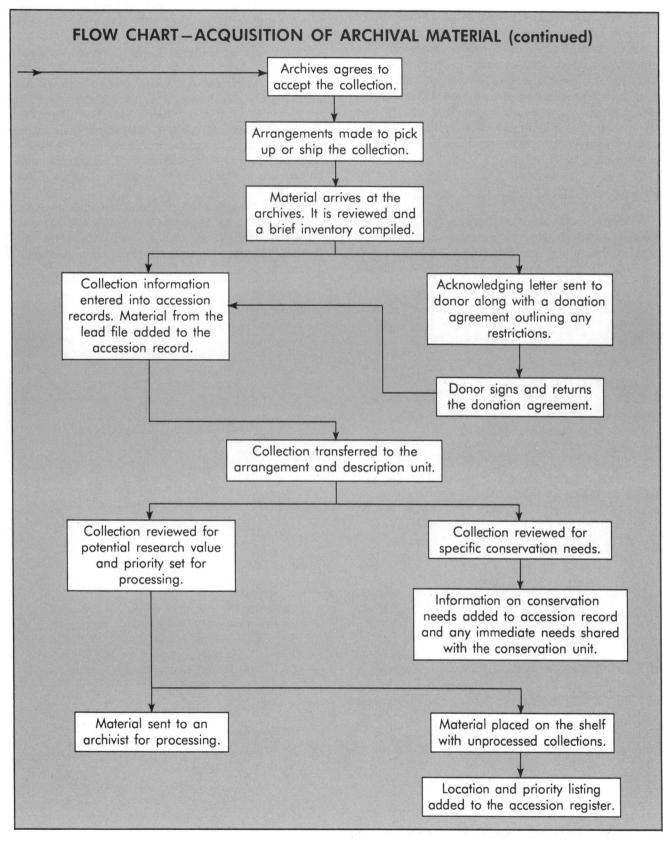

FLOW CHART—ACQUISITION OF ARCHIVAL MATERIAL (continued)

Conclusion

Organizational structure must be one of the archival administrator's top priorities. As archives grow larger and their tasks become more complex, organizational structures must be reviewed regularly to ensure continued effectiveness. Using planning techniques discussed in the next chapter, the structure will develop in response to demands upon the repository and be designed and built on the basis of a broad overview of the archives and its parent institution.

Suggested Readings

Organizational structure has not been dealt with in detail in archival literature. However, two places to begin are: Ann Pederson, *Keeping Archives* (Sydney, Australia: Australian Society of Archivists, 1987), pp. 21–27; and Kenneth W. Duckett, *Modern Manuscripts, A Practical Manual for Their Management, Care and Use* (Nashville: American Association for State and Local History, 1975), pp. 21–28.

Literature in related disciplines includes: Frederick L. Rath and Merrilyn Rogers O'Connell, *Bibliographies on Historical Organization Practices: Administration* (Nashville: American Association for State and Local History, 1980); Alan D. Ullberg and Patricia Ullberg, *Museum Trusteeship* (Washington, D.C.: American Association of Museums, 1981); and Marion Paquet, *A Handbook for Cultural Trustees* (Washington, D.C.: American Association of Museums, 1987).

Useful management literature includes: Andrew O. Manzini, *Organization Diagnosis* (Detroit: Gale Research, 1988); and J. Famularo, *Organizational Planning Manual* (Detroit: Gale Research, 1979).

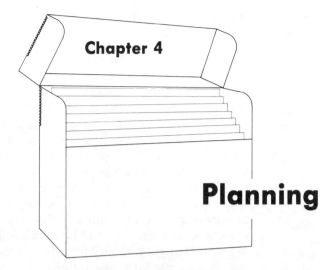

Chapter 4

Planning

The Importance of Planning

Strategic planning takes a broad view of the needs and aspirations of an archival program. As a management concept, planning was developed to focus on the needs of large, complex organizations, but planning is needed in institutions of all sizes. It enables them to use a wide range of human, monetary, and material resources to achieve certain specific goals. Planning is necessary and important because no institution has unlimited resources. With limited manpower and finances, a repository is constantly making choices: it can process one hundred cubic feet of records, or develop three new exhibits, or automate its finding aid system. It can react to current demands, or it can make choices in the context of its long-range needs and its overall plan. However decisions are made, there are risks since no one can foresee all consequences. Long-range planning cannot eliminate risk, but it can put choices into a broader context where the effects of certain decisions are seen in relationship to other choices and other results.

Planning as methodology developed primarily in the twentieth century, but it is a concept as old as mankind. As rational beings, humans have the ability to plan and organize complex tasks. Without these skills such monuments as the pyramids, the great gothic cathedrals of Europe, or the Eiffel Tower could not have been built. These achievements were not carried out using modern management planning but required a conceptualization and an approach which has become codified in twentieth-century planning techniques.

The American space program is an excellent example of strategic planning. It began in earnest after the launching of the Russian sputnik satellite in 1957. Stung by the Russian achievement, the federal government allocated extensive resources and developed detailed plans for an American space program. Its goal was to land a man on the moon, an achievement which was accomplished in only twelve years. The success of long-range planning in this example came from its focus on a specific vision, landing a man on the moon. This vision inspired those allocating funds for space exploration, the president and Congress, to continue their support. It also inspired those working directly and indirectly on the project and focused their energy toward one specific event. But the space program is also an example of an organization which lost its focus once that goal was achieved; some constituencies supported the space shuttle, others the skylab and interplanetary exploration. The loss of vision undermined congressional support, affected staff morale, and led to fighting within the space community. The role of goals and vision in planning cannot be overemphasized; it is central to developing a long-range plan.

Although the space program is perhaps one of the best examples of the value of planning in completing a complex task, planning is widely used in business, government, and the military. One of its primary values is its ability to focus individual or group attention on an entire task. In taking a global view of an institution, it allows the individual or group to consider a wide range of contingencies, develop a vision of the future, and establish specific goals which lead to achievement of the task. Both the designers of the pyramids and the leaders of the American space program had vision. Before beginning, they had an image in their minds of the final product and what it would achieve so they could direct their resources towards its creation. Vision is an integral part of planning, and without it, all planning concepts and procedures are of little value.

Archival Planning

Planning is important for every repository, regardless of size. Whether an archives has one staff member or one hundred, it faces demands greater than its available resources. Not all tasks can be done at the same time. Each requires a major effort, and the archives must decide which of the projects has the greatest priority. Planning will assist the repository in establishing priorities and will stake out a path which will lead to the completion of all tasks over time.

Planning is applicable to every institution, whether recently established or approaching its centennial. When a new program faces a wide range of demands, planning allows it to develop a set of priorities so that it can begin with the most critical tasks while maintaining an overview of what must ultimately be accomplished. For older repositories, planning provides a review of current activities. Such a review may indicate activities that are no longer useful or valid and can suggest changes needed to set and achieve new goals.

Planning generally follows a set pattern, which is illustrated in Figure 4-1.

Mission Statement

The planning process begins with a definition of the repository: what the archives is and what it does. This description is called a mission statement. It should answer a number of questions: Why does the repository exist? What does it do? Whom does it serve? Which is its parent organization, and what is its function? A mission statement sets the parameters for the repository and becomes the basis upon which all planning proceeds.

How does a person developing a plan answer these questions? Answers can be found in government statutes or legislation if the institution is a state or local government archives, while other types of archives might find such information in repository policy statements, organizational bylaws, institutional policies or minutes of the governing board. If guidance cannot be found in any of these sources, archivists must create a mission statement on the basis of their understanding of the repository's role and responsibility within the organization in consultation with the parent organization's administration and/or advisory board.

Once this basic research has been completed, the statement can be drafted. Mission statements are generally short, no more than a paragraph, and must be general if they are to cover all aspects of an archives' activities. A typical mission statement might read:

> The mission of the University Archives is to support the goals of Southern State University by identifying, collecting, preserving, and making available university

Figure 4-1   Planning Flow Chart

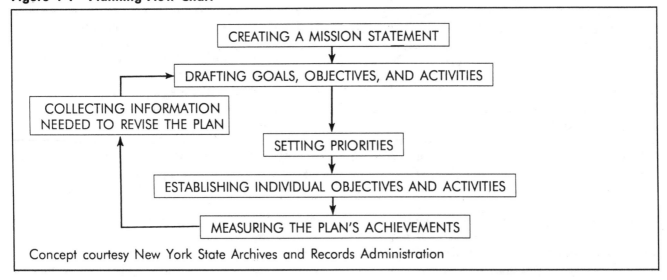

Concept courtesy New York State Archives and Records Administration

records and personal papers of enduring value from administrators, faculty, and students from 1889 to the present for the use of university staff, students, scholars, and the general public.

The mission statement answers four basic questions:

1. What groups, activities, or experiences does the archives document? Southern State University's.

2. Why was the program initiated? To identify, collect, preserve, and make available for use university records and personal papers.

3. What does the repository collect? University records and personal papers of enduring value from administrators, faculty, and students from 1889 to the present.

4. What groups or interests does it serve? Staff, students, scholars, and the general public.

The Planning Process

The planning process can begin in earnest when the mission statement is complete. Planning should not begin without the input and approval of the parent institution. Archival planners should be aware of institution-wide planning documents and should seek to place archival plans within that context. A long-range plan should cover a period of three to five years, which is probably the maximum time for which one can predict future changes and developments. Also, most plans currently envisaged should be accomplished in that length of time.

Planning is considered an administrative function but must involve all staff members. In a larger repository, a planning committee may draft a plan incorporating suggestions or plans from subcommittees representing departments or bureaus. As the planning process proceeds, continuing communication is needed from bottom to top and top to bottom. Full communication and consultation will insure that, once the plan is adopted, staff members will be aware of its value and have a stake in making it work.

In addition to staff involvement, the planning process should involve a variety of archival constituencies. These might include:

1. An archives advisory committee, if one exists.

2. Administrators outside the archives who have supervisory or administrative responsibility for its program.

3. Departments or researchers using the archives on a regular basis.

4. Records creators donating material to the collection.

Input from these groups will be extremely valuable since they view the repository from an outside perspective.

Institutional Analysis

Planning should begin with a review of the archives' history and its past achievements and shortcomings. This should include all aspects of the program: legal authority, governance, financial support, physical facilities, personnel, appraisal and records management, arrangement and description, reference and access, outreach, and preservation. (See Figure 4-2.) The study should take into consideration such issues as the length of time the archives has been established, and whether it is an institutional archives or a manuscript repository.

A review should indicate program strengths as well as focus on immediate and long-term needs of the organization. Information on past activities can come from such sources as annual or monthly reports, previous planning documents, budgets, and personnel reviews of individual employees. All should be carefully scrutinized. The collected information will be extremely helpful in the planning process and should help gauge what may reasonably be accomplished in the future. (See Figure 4-3.)

A successful plan must also examine the repository's internal and external environment, taking into account such factors as:

1. The level of financial and program support from the archives' parent institution.

2. The parent institution's long-range plan.

3. The program emphases and funding levels of grant-giving agencies.

4. Standards of archival practice.

5. Current developments in the profession.

6. Changes in record keeping and records technology.

When the planning process begins, the planning committee accepts certain assumptions as facts. These assumptions underlying the planning process should be identified in the plan so that readers are

Figure 4-2 Assessment Checklist

1. LEGAL AUTHORITY AND PURPOSE

Principles. "There must be explicit documentation of an archives' legal status and authority. The archives must have a formal statement of its purpose."

Amplification. To function effectively, an archives must have authority for its establishment, legal standing, and purpose. This authority should be stated explicitly in a formal document. The archives should also have a program statement describing the functions it must perform and the resources it needs to achieve its purposes.

YES   NO   N/A

____   ____   ____   1. Does the archives have a document or documents that authorize its establishment and continued existence?

____   ____   ____   2. Does the archives comply with legal requirements, if any, to maintain its authority and status?

____   ____   ____   3. Is the documentation that establishes the legal status of the archives sufficiently comprehensive and definitive?

____   ____   ____   4. Does the documentation clearly define the role and function of the archives?

____   ____   ____   5. Does the documentation clearly delineate the lines of authority and responsibility of the person in charge of the archives?

____   ____   ____   6. Is there within the same documentation a statement of purposes and objectives and the functions the archives is to perfom in fulfilling them?

____   ____   ____   7. Are the objectives and functions stated clearly, and do they embody and reflect nationally accepted archival principles and functions?

____   ____   ____   8. Can the archives' performance of its functions be compared to the purposes and objectives so as to arrive at a reasonable appraisal of success or failure?

____   ____   ____   9. Does the person responsible for the archives have sufficient authority to ensure that the archives performs its functions so as to meet its objectives?

____   ____   ____   10. If the archives is part of a larger institution, is the archives' statement of purpose consonant with the purposes of the institution?

Archives Assessment and Planning Workbook (SAA, 1989) p. 16.

aware of them. Many variables affect a plan and these should be clarified as much as possible. Examples of such assumptions might include:

1. The archives budget will increase at a rate of 5 percent per year.
2. Increased storage space planned for the archives will be completed in twelve months.
3. Staffing levels will remain constant during the long-range plan.

Developing Goals, Objectives, and Activities

When developing a plan for a repository, the staff should focus its thinking into general categories connected with the repository's work: acquisition and appraisal, arrangement and description, reference and access, preservation, outreach, and general administration. Within these specific categories, the archives should develop a hierarchical plan using standard management terminology. The terms most commonly used are goals, objectives, and activities. Using a hierarchical model, members of the staff can see the long-term results for which they are striving, the intermediate steps to achieve those ends, and the specific steps they need to take in order make the plan work.

Goals, the broadest category, are action oriented and grow from the mission statement. They provide general direction for the repository and

Figure 4-3 Planning Worksheet

SECTION: LEGAL AUTHORITY AND PURPOSE

PROGRAM STRENGTHS:

1. _____

2. _____

3. _____

AREAS TO IMPROVE:

1. _____

NEXT ACTIONS: 1. _____

                 2. _____

                 3. _____

      STAFF RESP.: _____

      START DATE: _____ COMP. DATE: _____

2. _____

NEXT ACTIONS: 1. _____

                 2. _____

                 3. _____

      STAFF RESP.: _____

      START DATE: _____ COMP. DATE: _____

3. _____

NEXT ACTIONS: 1. _____

                 2. _____

                 3. _____

      STAFF RESP.: _____

      START DATE: _____ COMP. DATE: _____

Archives Assessment and Planning Workbook (SAA, 1989) p. 18.

---

should take a number of years to achieve. Goals should reflect current archival needs and should be based upon the research and study done by the planning team.

Examples of goals are:

1. Develop a cost-effective finding aid system which meets the needs of the repository clientele.

2. Create an acquisition program which reflects the goals of the parent institution and meets the needs of researchers.

3. Establish a sound financial policy and administrative base for the archival program.

Objectives are more specific actions in an archival plan and must be achieved to reach identified goals. Objectives should be measurable and be accomplished within a limited period of time. Objectives for the goal of creating an acquisition program might include:

1. Develop a collecting policy, taking into account the needs of the parent institution, the archives' geographical location, and comparable collections in other repositories.
2. Develop policies, procedures, and legal documents to ensure the systematic transfer of records from donors to the repository.
3. Establish collecting priorities and assign staff to acquisition responsibilities.

Objectives are more specific than goals and can be broken down into a number of smaller parts. These smaller units are called **activities**. They are finite projects which are carried out over a specific period of time, generally less than one year. Activities should be measurable and are generally assigned to one staff member to complete. Examples of activities to meet the objective to develop policies, procedures, and legal documents include:

1. Draft donor and transfer documentation in conjunction with appropriate legal counsel.
2. Develop standard access policies covering archival collections.
3. Establish a range of donor restrictions which the repository is prepared to accept.
4. Create accession and receipt forms and establish corresponding procedures.
5. Establish donor files and procedures covering the documentation of donations.
6. Establish a "lead file" for information on ongoing negotiations with potential donors.

Developing an Action Plan

During the planning process the staff should review all aspects of the archival program and formulate goals, objectives, and activities for all areas. This should result in a list of activities which can be achieved only if the optimum resources are available. Archival managers would like to attack all of their problems simultaneously, but limited personnel and/or financial resources usually preclude such a broad-based approach.

It is imperative that the archives develop a list of priorities which grow out of the overall plan. Ob-

jectives and activities with a lower priority can be accomplished at a later time when the items at the top of the priority list are completed. Developing a list of priorities must reflect the repository's current situation: its staffing level, its budgetary and institutional support, the quality and education of its staff, and the length of time it has been in existence. How do these factors influence the priorities in a given plan? If an archives has recently been established, its first priorities must be the development of overall policies and procedures. The repository should not begin collecting archives and manuscripts until it has written a collection policy, nor should it process records until it establishes arrangement and description standards and develops procedures for use on an ongoing basis.

Staff and funding levels can also play a major role in selecting planning priorities. If one of the first concerns is a lack of either staff or funds, then a high priority must be fund raising. Efforts must be concentrated on identifying sources of funds, developing means of increasing institutional funding, or developing outside grant support. If funding levels are adequate, the quality and education of the current staff will play a factor in choosing priorities. Planning should use the strength of individual staff members in appropriate areas and not waste useful resources. Staff strengths and interests should not be the only criteria in selecting priorities, but they should not be ignored.

Staff Involvement in Planning

Archival administrators should be aware that not all staff members will embrace planning with enthusiasm. Because planning implies both a review of current activities and the possibility of change, the staff may be fearful or anxious. These negative attitudes must be overcome through a continuing program of explanation and employee involvement in the planning process. Failure to involve staff may undermine the planning process and the entire effort will have been in vain. If planning is to be effective, staff members must understand the planning process and their role in the plan. While not everyone can be involved in all levels of the planning process, all staff members should be kept informed of developments and receive periodic updates.

Objectives and activities are generally of the most immediate importance to staff members since they relate directly to staff responsibilities. Objectives should be stated so they can be measured, and success or failure can be evaluated. Staff must also understand who is responsible for each objective and activity.

In addition to contributing to the larger plan, all employees should develop a list of individual objectives and activities which grow out of the larger organizational plan. These tasks should be both measurable and achievable. Staff will develop a personal commitment to overall institutional goals and objectives and work to gain their achievement if they can relate individual tasks to an overall plan. Developing individual objectives and activities will enable the staff to direct their energies toward their specific responsibilities. Individual objectives and activities also provide objective measurements of each employee for annual personnel evaluations and reviews of employee achievements.

Setting individual objectives and activities can be done both individually and collectively. Group planning can be done jointly by the entire staff in a smaller archives or by department members in a larger institution. Planning meetings are best held on days when other work can be set aside so that staff can give their full attention to the planning process. One or more days can be allocated to institutional planning, and such work should be done in a conference or meeting room away from the office, or in a retreat setting if adequate funding is available.

The focus of this meeting is planning, and an open format which involves planning exercises, group interaction, games, and meals may have other useful and positive effects on staff morale and cohesiveness. The goal of the meeting is to set individual objectives and activities, but useful by-products may include improved archival procedures, improved interpersonal relations among some or all staff members, and a better understanding of overall goals. If such meetings are to be successful, they must be carefully structured and timed. Regimentation is not the goal, and a balanced mixture of work, fun, and fellowship are needed to achieve a positive end. Although such meetings cannot be held more than once or twice a year, staff should meet for an hour or two on a monthly or bimonthly basis for updates on planning developments. These meetings can include some of the same components of the larger meeting to keep the spirit developed at the larger meeting alive.

After the group meeting is over, meetings should be held between supervisors and employees to agree on responsibilities for specific goals and activities. In addition, there should be a timetable or schedule indicating the completion dates for specific tasks. Work should be reviewed on a weekly, monthly, or quarterly basis to ensure that work is progressing toward completion. Delays or unanticipated problems should be discussed by the employee and supervisor, and new deadlines set once problems are resolved.

Revising and Updating the Plan

Planning is a continuous process. Plans are only plans and must adapt to changes in the archives' environment: changes in funding, staffing, or responsibilities will affect the long-range plan. For the plan to evolve and meet changes in the institutional environment, the staff must develop reporting systems which collect data on when and how the objectives and activities are being completed. This data should be collected at all archival levels so there can be a continual adjustment in both individual and institutional objectives. Such information can be collected as part of ongoing weekly, monthly, or quarterly reports. If, however, such a reporting structure does not already exist, then a system must be created so that the planning document can change to meet current needs. Reports from employees to supervisors and higher administrators will indicate progress on specific projects listed on the plan and indicate when they have been completed. Such reporting is especially necessary where complex projects are involved or where a project continues over a number of years, and each part of the project must be completed in a particular sequence.

With the availability of information on the plan's progress, an administrator and staff can revise the plan to reflect current staffing, financial resources, and outside events. Minor changes in the plan may be needed on a quarterly or semi-annual basis, but a more complete review will be needed at the end of every year. Short-range plans will involve most members of the staff and should be done after the completion of the annual report and the compilation of annual statistics. With this information in hand, there can be a thorough review of the long-range plan and adjustments can be made reflecting the repository's current situation.

Conclusion

For the archival manager, planning is a necessity. To develop a balanced archival program, the archivist must have an overview of all archival functions. Planning provides a framework to review all programs and insure balanced development over time. Planning serves both to remind and to prod archivists to accomplish needed tasks. It is, in reality, nothing more than a sophisticated list of tasks which can be checked off as they are completed. If thinking of planning in this context makes it easier to practice, then by all means think of it as a list. However one conceives of the planning process, the most important step is to begin. Achievement cannot begin without planning, and without achievement, archival programs will not receive the support they need. Planning will allow archives to achieve their goals on a rational and timely basis. Once started, archivists will wonder how they ever got along without planning.

Suggested Readings

In developing archival plans, administrators must evaluate all program aspects before planning future activities. The following volumes will be of assistance in carrying out this task: Society of American Archivists, *Evaluation of Archival Institutions: Services, Principles, and Guide to Self-Study* (Chicago: Society of American Archivists, 1982). Paul H. McCarthy, ed., *Archives Assessment and Planning Workbook* (Chicago: Society of American Archivists,

1989). New York State Archives and Records Administration, *Strengthening New York's Historical Records Programs: A Self-Study Guide* (Albany: New York State Archives and Records Administration, 1989).

Two useful examples of planning documents are Society of American Archivists, *Planning for the Archival Profession, A Report of the SAA Task Force on Goals and Priorities* (Chicago: Society of American Archivists, 1986); and Delaware Historical Records Advisory Board, *Delaware's Documentary Heritage: The Future of Historical Records in The First State* (Dover: Delaware Historical Records Advisory Board, 1986).

For additional information on planning, see Hedy A. Hartman and Suzanne B. Schell, "Institutional Master Planning for Historical Organizations and Museums," *Technical Report 11* (Nashville: American Association for State and Local History, 1986); Bruce W. Dearstyne, "Planning for Archival Programs: An Introduction," MARAC Technical Leaflet No. 3, *Mid-Atlantic Regional Archivist* 12 (Summer 1983); and Robert Simerly, "Strategic Long-Range Planning," *Museum News* 58 (July/August 1980).

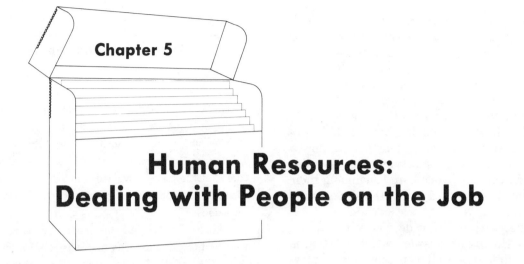

Chapter 5

Human Resources: Dealing with People on the Job

Over the years, the term "personnel management" has at least been partially replaced by "human resource management." The newer term points to significant developments in the way management studies have approached the issue of people at work. The idea that people often represent a manager's most valuable resource has become far more than a platitude.

A major turning point came in the 1960s with the development of Douglas McGregor's "Theory X/Theory Y" analysis.[1] Theory X described personnel management directed from the "top down" within an organization, with subordinates considered as little more than tools executing management's instructions. Theory Y defined a less authoritarian style which treated subordinates as active contributors in achieving an organization's goals. McGregor's studies have been thoroughly integrated into contemporary management philosophy and seem particularly appropriate in settings, such as archives, where managers must deal with employees who by virtue of education and experience consider themselves professionals worthy of a fair measure of autonomy and status.

Human resource management also suggests that human relations on the job involve more than the supervision of subordinates. The manager operates in a complex human environment, dealing with superiors and peers, as well as with subordinates. One authority has gone so far as to say that a manag-

er's principal job is "managing the boss," a term that will be discussed below. Finally, of course, the manager must manage himself or herself, a topic covered in Chapter 2.

Beginning with supervisory relationships, how does one manage people on the job? First, the manager must know which authority ultimately defines acceptable personnel practice in a given institution or organization. Though smaller institutions may have a less formal set of authorities with which to deal than do federal, state, or university archives or repositories, no archival repository will truly be independent of oversight and regulation of its personnel policies.

Second, the manager, from both pragmatic and ethical perspectives, must appreciate that the "human resource" is a person, governed by drives and needs that are complex and variable. The successful manager must balance the equal treatment of employees in matters where equity is preeminent, with the recognition that people must be treated as individuals. Though simple to state, putting this into practice can prove difficult.

Policies and Practices

Setting Goals. Successful personnel management requires actions and policies that relate to an organization's overall objectives. Management by habit may work for awhile, especially if an organization finds itself in a stable, noncompetitive environment, but it is at best a strategy for survival rather than growth. People are conscious of the objectives set for them; unlike the other resources with which

---

[1] Douglas McGregor, *The Human Side of Enterprise* (New York: McGraw-Hill, 1960). This book remains a seminal work on human resource management.

a manager must deal, people have their own objectives, of which achievement or satisfaction in the workplace will be only a part. People need goals, both to provide a purpose for their efforts and to serve as standards for measuring performance. One of the advantages archival managers are likely to have over their counterparts in other organizations is the strong dedication archivists have to their profession. Archival managers must articulate how a repository contributes to preserving the past, but they should not have to work hard convincing their staffs that they are engaged in an ethical, valuable, public endeavor.

Job Description. What do you want an employee to do? Having an answer to this question is essential for current as well as prospective employees, for superiors, and for the manager. At some point employees are going to be evaluated on their performance, and it violates every rule of equity and good sense to evaluate them on any standard other than the description of the job they agreed to do. Managers need to create job descriptions and revise them as circumstances of employment change. (See Figure 5-1.)

Formulating a job advertisement from a job description is relatively simple. The duties and qualifications outlined in the advertisement must accurately reflect the job description. One area in which employers frequently choose to be somewhat secretive in advertisements is salary. "Salary and benefits competitive and commensurate with qualifications," or some variant, is a common phrase in professional advertisements—perhaps too common. Though employers may argue that they need to retain flexibility in such matters, is there any harm in including at least a salary range in the advertisement?

Additional information required in an advertisement include:

Point of Contact: To whom should applicants apply? What documents (resume, references, etc.) should accompany the initial inquiry? Where further information is available, a phone number should be supplied.

Closing Date: What is the deadline for applications?

Recruitment. How should a manager fill a vacancy? That seems simple enough: "With the best person available!" But life is rarely so simple. First of all, a manager needs to know what institutional limitations or restrictions exist in hiring. Does the head of the archives have the authority to hire or only to recommend a candidate? Do regulations give preference to current employees? In larger organiza-

Figure 5-1

Writing a Job Description

BASIC INFORMATION: What is the position? Where is it located?

DUTIES: This section should include the principle activities associated with the job. It should identify the incumbent's role in each activity. "Directs," "manages," "appraises," and "is responsible for" are useful terms; "is involved with" is not. To whom does the person report? Is supervisory responsibility included?

QUALIFICATIONS: What education or experience is required for the job? Can one substitute for the other? What qualifications are preferred rather than required? In setting qualifications for professional jobs, what standards will apply? Repositories may develop their own criteria, or they may be forced to use those prescribed in a personnel or civil service code. Though the development of professional and educational standards for archivists remains incomplete, repositories would seem negligent in ignoring the efforts at definition that have been put forth.[2]

SALARY: This may be a precise figure, a range, a pay grade, or range of grades. Where a range is permitted, management must make clear what criteria determine placement and advancement within the range.

SPECIAL CIRCUMSTANCES: Is this a temporary, grant-funded, or permanent position?

---

tions, what role does the personnel office play? Does the organization have and use written job standards for archivists? Managers may wish to develop such standards, utilizing information from professional sources and organizations, especially if recruiting actions are likely to be frequent or numerous.

The search for "the best person available" requires familiarity with collective bargaining agreements (where they exist) and affirmative action plans. The former may mandate a preference for hiring from within, with emphasis on seniority. The latter may reinforce such considerations, but could in fact be in contention with them, encouraging an external search to redress demonstrated imbalances

---

[2] Information on standards for institutions offering archival training and on the professional certification of archivists is available from the Society of American Archivists and from regional archival organizations.

Figure 5-2

Job descriptions and job advertisements will differ in format and purpose; nonetheless, they must both present an accurate description of a position's essential responsibilities.

Society of American Archivists
Education Officer/Senior Archivist

JOB DESCRIPTION

(This is an abbreviated version of the job description for Education Officer/Senior Archivist.)

Education Officer (50% of duties)

1. Generally responsible for successful completion of NHPRC/Mellon-funded project to expand continuing professional education for archivists:
   - consults with the Advisory Committee and Executive Director;
   - manages project budget and regular financial reports;
   - develops and oversees all activities undertaken as part of the project:
     —solicits and evaluates proposals for workshops;
     —selects workshop instructors;
   - supervises and evaluates Program Assistant and other staff directly involved in NHPRC/Mellon project;
   - provides liaison with various SAA groups.
2. Responsible for administering all other SAA educational programs:
   - assists Executive Director in supervising Program Officers for such other projects as may be funded;
   - reviews SAA's educational offerings.
3. Supervises preparation of annual SAA Education Directory.

Senior Archivist (50%)

1. Assists Executive Director in providing information about archival topics.
2. Assists Executive Director in maintaining contact with regional archival organizations.
5. Reviews drafts of potential SAA publications.
8. Serves as deputy for Executive Director as needed.
9. Other duties as assigned.

JOB ADVERTISEMENT

EDUCATION OFFICER AND SENIOR ARCHIVIST

SAA is seeking an experienced and qualified archivist to direct the Society's expanding program of continuing education opportunities, and to perform other duties. The Education Officer is responsible for scheduling and promoting SAA's existing short courses and workshops; for designing and developing additional educational offerings; for evaluating, supporting, and improving all of these educational services; and for supervising SAA's special initiatives in preservation, automation, and related areas. The Education Officer works with instructors, regional archival associations, the Committee on Education and Professional Development, and others to ensure that the Society's educational program is professionally and financially successful. The Education Officer also assists the Program Committee in developing the annual meeting program, directs the Society's employment services, takes on special assignments, provides staff support for certain SAA groups, and assists in the overall operation of the SAA office. This is a full-time, permanent position in the Society's Chicago office. Salary is expected to be in the mid-30s. Available November 1, 1989. Send applications and nominations to Executive Director, Society of American Archivists, 600 S. Federal St., Suite 504, Chicago, Illinois 60605 before September 15, 1989.

Though the *responsibilities* outlined in this example are comparable, the emphasis in the advertisement is placed heavily on the *duties* as education officer. This is clearly what the employer intends and is consistent with the principle that descriptions and advertisement should not conflict. The size and budget of many archival institutions will require employees to perform multiple functions, including the ever present "other duties as assigned," but indicating a primary emphasis is appropriate, even if, as in this example, the duties are formally divided on a "50-50" basis.

in the composition of the current staff. Collective bargaining agreements, merit promotion laws, and affirmative action programs can also influence or determine where and how a vacancy is advertised.

Given the range of considerations that must be taken into account, recruiting can be a complicated process. In many respects it should be, for few managerial functions have equivalent impact on an organization.

Once these considerations have been dealt with, the manager needs a recruiting strategy. How should the position be filled? By informally recruiting individuals known to the manager, by posting notices on the bulletin boards in local universities, or by such professional devices as the SAA employment bulletin, regional newsletters, and the like? Managers may not need to use "all of the above" in each instance, but they should have a clear understanding of why they have chosen a particular strategy in a given instance.

Applications. The handling of applications requires certain guidelines. First, resumes and similar documents are personal, privileged information; they must be handled with discretion. Next, an applicant is entitled to a response to the application—acknowledging its receipt and giving information on the sequence and schedule that will follow.

The first step in reviewing applications is to confirm the information supplied and expand on it through communication with references. The manager can bring staff members into the selection process by having them assist in the review or interview processes, a step that can broaden the perspective applied to applicant selection.

Next, the manager will select those applicants who merit an interview, first by eliminating applicants who do not meet the qualifications for the job. The manager may then cull even further, looking for those applicants who most clearly exceed the minimal requirements. Ultimately, assuming an interview phase is to be part of the selection process, the manager will have available a "short list" of interviewees.

Interviewing and Hiring

The purpose of the hiring interview is to find a candidate whose education, experience, and interests qualify him or her for the job advertised. The interviewer needs to find out whether the candidate meets the specifications for the job. The interviewer also needs to provide the candidate with information—beyond that which is contained in the job de-

scription—about the organization for which the candidate is applying. A candidate is a bit like the Czarist refugee who showed up at a London bank to deposit his fortune. When asked for references, the refugee replied, "Pardon me, this is my money. Where are *your* references?" The candidate is, in fact, being asked to make as much of an investment as the potential employer.

Preparing for and Conducting the Interview. The interviewer needs knowledge about the job being filled and the organization of which it is part, and knowledge of the candidate's credentials. The interviewer should attempt to standardize interviews for the same job to ensure that each candidate is treated fairly. This serves not only the candidates, but also the organization. It does no one any good to have a potentially excellent employee excluded because of a premature, subjective decision.

Subjectivity is a fact of life. Appearance and demeanor count, and there is no reason, legal or otherwise, why they should not. Such factors need to be related to the job (a reference archivist probably needs better "people skills" than does a preservation technician), and they need to be balanced against all the other factors the candidate brings to a position.

What cannot be considered are preconceptions based on age, sex, race, or religion. Physical impairment may be taken into account only when the impairment is directly related to the candidate's ability to perform the job. Organizations need to ensure that managers and others involved in the hiring process do not apply discriminatory standards of intelligence, appearance, and personality. For example, are certain character traits, such as aggressiveness or assertiveness, considered to be assets for men but not for women?

Setting. The interview should be conducted in a setting that permits both candidate and interviewer to be at their best. Privacy and freedom from interruption are important. The burden of setting the tone for the interview rests on the interviewer, who must attempt to establish a warm but professional climate in which communication is encouraged. Something as simple as a friendly greeting and handshake can go a long way toward making the interview work. The interviewer should then inform the candidate what information he or she has seen and define the objectives for the interview.

Information Exchange. The interview must do more than review information already available from resumes and transcripts. Why, if the job is substantially different from previous experience, is the candidate applying for the open position? Diversification per se is a valid reason ("I just think I need a change."), but a positive interest in diversifying toward a given area, rather than simply away from a stale environment, is even better.

Beyond simply qualifying for the advertised position, does the candidate express interests that are likely to be fulfilled in the job? Candidates who say the most satisfying aspect of their career is dealing with researchers should be questioned on their interest in a job which promises little contact of that sort.

One question that will surely come up in an interview is salary, which in some cases will be set by law or other authority. Even in these instances, however, the interviewer can address other benefits and the prospects for promotion or increases in salary. The interviewer must make clear to the applicant what considerations will be included in a salary determination, who will make that decision, and when a firm offer will be made. No applicant should ever be asked to accept a job offer with the assurance that "we'll work out the salary details later."

The candidate should be encouraged to ask questions or provide information that either the application or the interview may have missed. The candidate should understand the selection process and be given a reasonable estimate of the time it will take. If the interview is held at the repository, a tour, the opportunity to meet members of the staff, and access to copies of appropriate guides or other publications can be helpful.

After the Interview. The interviewer must evaluate the candidate's performance, preferably on a form standardized for use with all candidates. An initial evaluation of the candidate's strengths and weaknesses should be included, but candidates should not be ranked until all candidates have completed the process.

Once a choice is made, the selected candidate should be notified and provided with procedures for responding to the selection, reporting dates, and so forth. If the candidate is relocating, procedures (if any) for assisting in that process should be provided. Applicants who are not selected should be notified and thanked for their interest. In organizations large enough to have frequent vacancies, the manager may offer to keep a candidate's application on file.

Directing/Supervising

Supervision involves applying personnel resources to the tasks for which a manager's unit or organization is responsible. Employees must be informed of the organization's objectives and of their duties in relation to those objectives. The manager is responsible for the continuous monitoring of performance (of systems and other resources, as well as personnel) in pursuit of those objectives. As goals and objectives are reviewed, the manager needs to ensure that employees have the opportunity and means to contribute to that review.

The effective manager will communicate observations to higher management as well as to the workforce. Whether formal or informal, communication, as noted elsewhere, is fundamental to effective management. Managers who communicate effectively will have far fewer problems than those who do not. This means both transmitting information to staff members and receiving information from them. Nothing will frustrate the success of an organization more completely than employees who feel that they cannot approach management with their ideas or with their sense that something is not working properly.

With any luck, the manager will be communicating good news of objectives met, work accomplished, and goals exceeded. The manager needs to see that the persons responsible for such accomplishments are recognized and rewarded. The form of such recognition may depend on available resources, but the absence of resources should never be an excuse for not providing recognition. Letters of appreciation and "staff member of the month" programs are intangible, but they work, especially if the recipients are made to feel that management's actions represent a genuine desire to recognize a job well done.

Performance Review

Performance evaluation, and communication about performance, is a continuous process. From time to time, most often on an annual basis, this process is formalized in a performance review or appraisal. The effective manager will ensure that the annual review does not substitute for ongoing communication. A manager's responsibilities to direct and develop employees is not fulfilled by a thirty-minute annual performance review.

A performance review should include three elements: an assessment of the employee's performance during the rating period being reviewed, an evaluation of the employee's potential for development within the organization, and consideration of a plan to permit the employee to obtain the additional skills, education, or experience needed to realize that potential. Reviews help the employer to obtain the level of employee performance needed to achieve the

Figure 5-3

The Self-Appraisal Technique

One technique for assisting in performance appraisal is to have employees evaluate themselves, using the same form and criteria employed by their supervisor. Self-appraisal can then be part of the evaluation process, providing the employee's perspective on his or her own performance. Everyone involved needs to understand, of course, that the supervisor's appraisal, possibly modified to reflect information supplied by the employee, is the one that counts. It is not unlikely that managers will find employees rating themselves at lower levels than those provided by the manager. Whether higher or lower, self-appraisals can illustrate differences between management's perception and employee perceptions on such areas as definition of responsibilities and priorities, as well as on performance itself. Managers using this technique need to make clear that their appraisals do not consider employees in isolation (a common problem with self-appraisals), but relative to other employees with comparable skill, experience, and professional status.

organization's goals and to improve the level of employee performance. For the employee, the performance review should provide a sense of knowing where he or she stands, from management's viewpoint, as well as highlight areas in which present skills need to be improved or new abilities acquired.

An effective review or appraisal program will only result from the creation and adoption of standards for performance, tied specifically to *the job the employee was assigned to do.* Hiring one person as an archivist, and requiring graduate education and appropriate experience, then hiring another as a technician (requiring less experience and education) and evaluating both according to identical standards makes no sense.

Standards can be set for such factors as the amount of work performed (how many records should be reviewed, for example), the employee's knowledge of the job, the degree of decision making and autonomy associated with the job, the employee's skill in communicating (orally or in writing), and even the employee's attitude (initiative, enthusiasm, etc.). Employees must know in advance the factors on which they will be rated.

Before presenting the appraisal, the manager should review the process by which it was derived.

Is the appraisal consistent with appraisals given to other employees? Does it reflect a fair, accurate summary of the employee's performance? Or does it lean too heavily upon the most recent significant event or development involving the employee? Employees being rated for a twelve-month period should be rated for the whole period, not just on the basis of a recent success or disaster. Managers need to be certain that they are evaluating performance, not their relationship with the employee; they must be certain that the facts used in the appraisal are accurate; and they must balance negative aspects with a review of areas in which the employee has performed acceptably. Presenting the appraisal to the employee, working with the employee to establish a plan for the employee's future development, and agreeing on goals and essential duties for the next appraisal period complete the formal appraisal.

A performance review in which communication is one-way—from the supervisor to the employee—is a lost opportunity. (See Figure 5-3.) How does the employee feel about the last year's performance? What ideas does the employee have to enhance both personal performance and the overall performance of the organization? What would he or she like to be doing three years from now? What steps (training, diversification) would be needed to get ready for that position?

Such questions ought not be asked only during the annual performance review. Managers who allow this to happen will have turned an essential and rewarding part of supervision into an empty formality. Continuous communication between manager and employees provides more effective correction of performance problems, and should reduce, if not eliminate, the element of uncertainty that can make appraisal interviews difficult.

Training and Development

If people are an organization's most important resource, it follows that they should be treated with due regard for the human potential for change and growth. Every organization, no matter how small, needs a program for staff development—even if the staff consists only of one archivist.

Employee development programs can encompass extensive training efforts, conferences, and seminars. But they can begin simply, with a statement from the organization of its policies toward employee development. Will the organization reimburse employees for training or membership in professional organizations? At a minimum, can the in-

An archivist helps to train archives staff members in the use of computers. *(Barbara B. Taylor, courtesy Department of Archives and History, State of Alabama)*

stitution's budget permit employees to be paid while attending professional meetings? Does the organization provide access to professional literature? Is information on meetings and workshops run by SAA, regional organizations, or by the parent institution posted or otherwise brought to the attention of staff members?

Limited resources can determine the shape and extent of a career development program; they should not be excuses for their absence. Many workshops and conferences are available at nominal cost, and employees should expect to shoulder at least part of the burden for education and other opportunities for which they, as much as their employers, are the beneficiary. In some cases, an organization's only support to employees seeking an advanced degree or other training may be time off the job to attend class.

The benefits of career development should be especially attractive to archival institutions, which invest heavily in skills developed only after long experience with a collection, its donors, and its researchers. Employee turnover will occur under the best of circumstances, but for an archives to lose personnel because a job has been outgrown and management has made no plans for career development can be especially painful. While an employee may be replaced with someone with equivalent or even superior credentials, the institution will still have suffered a loss.

Career development efforts need to be geared to the varying career levels of employees. Clerical and technical personnel may be interested in developmental opportunities in their fields, but they may also be interested in acquiring the credentials necessary for professional status. Professionals, especially those with advanced degrees, place extremely high value on independence, and development programs need to reflect this. Sabbaticals or programs permitting interested staff members time off for writing or research are valuable both to the institution and to the profession as a whole. Institutions have an obligation, within resource limits, to encourage staff members to participate actively in the meetings and publications that are the center of any profession's being. Because the average archival institution is far removed from the size and breadth of Fortune 500 companies, opportunities for promotion, not to mention significant monetary remuneration, for archivists can be limited. Archival managers can, realistically, do little to change this. They can, however, encourage the growth of skills and experience that will enhance the archivist's sense of participation and contribution in his or her chosen field.

Helping Employees Succeed

Most managers find personnel problems to be the most difficult they must face. Leaky roofs and inadequate budgets are one thing; dealing with a poorly performing or disgruntled employee is something else entirely. Most repository staffs are small in size, and the employee whose performance is in question may well be a longtime colleague or friend, making the situation even more difficult. How should the manager proceed?

Deficient performance can result from a number of causes. Is the employee capable of doing the assigned job? Are the tools—including training—provided to the employee sufficient to permit a job's successful completion? Are the duties set forth in the job description realistic, both in the amount and level of work required of the employee?

Before assuming that an employee is failing because of his or her inadequacies, management needs to make sure that it is not assisting failure or making it inevitable. Has some circumstance, internal or external, rendered the employee's job description out of date? Suppose management has implemented a successful outreach program that, over a short period of time, doubles the number of researchers using a repository. Has the increase in the number of researchers using the repository made it impossible for the reference staff to perform its functions? Has the decision to accept a valuable but deteriorating collection forced a preservation staff to put aside routine or previously scheduled work?

Once the problem has been identified, the manager must devise a remedy. Is training available to correct deficiencies? Can other personnel be assigned, even part-time, to assist an overburdened colleague, at least until it can be determined that the increased workload is not an aberration?

If the manager determines that the problem lies with an employee, he or she should arrange to discuss it with that person. This can be an uncomfortable step for both manager and employee, but several guidelines may help:

1. Focus on performance, not personality.
2. Within reason, recognize that doing things differently is not the same as doing things poorly.
3. Reserve judgment until the employee has had a chance to explain his or her view of the situation.
4. Invite the employee to suggest ways to rectify the situation.
5. In both word and behavior, emphasize a preference for encouraging success, not noting failure.

The last point is critical. Employees' reactions to counseling may depend far more on how they think the manager feels about them than on the specific issues discussed. Is the manager out to encourage employees to do better? Or is the emphasis on restating who's in charge? Is the manager willing to listen to what an employee has to say? Or has the manager already reached a judgment on the matter under discussion?

This is not a choice between being a nice person and being an effective manager. No manager can guarantee that employees will approve of every management decision. Managers *can* enhance the likelihood that employees will respect those decisions by creating a work environment in which mutual respect for all members of the staff is encouraged, along with a dedication to achieving common goals.

What about the possibility of personal problems? Generally, these are of no concern to the manager, unless work is disturbed through chronic absence or lateness, lengthy phone conversations at the work site, or the employee's inability to put aside personal problems on the job.

Accepting a management position does not, however, involve resigning from the human race. Managers should be sympathetic to an employee undergoing personal stress. Deaths of loved ones, illness in the family, and personal disappointments happen to everyone. Moreover, even in the most bureaucratic situations, people establish personal contacts and relationships with their co-workers, includ-

ing their bosses. Managers must be realistic in assessing the degree to which subordinates will bring their personal lives into the workplace, and equally realistic in expecting that even the most conscientious employee will encounter periods of reduced effectiveness. Managers must also recognize that their subordinates are also colleagues (and even friends), and they should not be unwilling to react to them in those capacities.

At some point, however, the manager may need to counsel an employee whose performance has declined, perhaps as the result of personal problems. The manager may even suggest that the employee consider seeking assistance from personal or social service providers available either within the organization or from the community at large. Personnel offices in large organizations should be equipped either to provide or to make referrals for a wide range of services.

Managers need to keep in mind the limits of both their authority and their capabilities in counseling employees. Every large organization has its share of office therapists, but this role needs to be approached carefully. The manager who crosses beyond clearly determined limits in performing such functions runs the risk of seeing his own effectiveness reduced, and perhaps even of making a difficult situation worse.

Effective managers create a climate in which members of an organization share a sense of contribution and participation in the organization's mission. In such a climate, most discipline should be the self-discipline of people sharing in a cooperative effort, under conditions and practices they see as conducive to that effort. This objective is most likely to be met where communication on goals and procedures is encouraged, and where employees feel free to participate in their development. Edwards Deming, one of the foremost management consultants of the postwar era, has said that management's job is to create a climate in which "everyone may take joy in their work," a sentiment that managers should keep in mind in directing the workplace. Managers who find themselves spending much of their time *solving* problems with employees should consider whether they have put enough emphasis on *preventing* problems.

Managing Professionals

The archival manager may have to deal with a full range of clerical, technical, and professional personnel. Without slighting the needs of the first two categories, the nature of the archival profession requires some attention to be paid to the last. By their years of training and their adherence to an occupation providing a valuable public service, archivists consider themselves professionals who, like other "salaried professionals," can present managers with serious challenges. A desire for autonomy, a disdain for close supervision, and a desire to defend professional technique from what are often seen as the insensitive intrusions of management are among the attitudes many professionals bring to the job.

Occasional clashes of managerial and professional cultures may be unavoidable, but they can be controlled. The fact that most archival managers are archivists should help, though some subordinates may see acceptance of a managerial position as evidence of a lack of dedication or commitment to the "true" profession. Managers, whether they share an archival background or not, need to assure the professionals in their employ that decisions involving professional integrity will not be overridden by managerial considerations. In larger organizations, dual track career systems (one track based on professional achievement, the other on management) can reduce the problems that result when skilled professionals feel forced into management positions as their only route to advancement.

Volunteers and Interns

Most archival institutions depend to one degree or another on adjunct employees, whether in the form of interns or volunteers. These can be extremely valuable staff members, stretching the limited resources available to most repositories. In many respects, adjunct interns should be managed like other members of the staff, with appropriate attention paid to those areas in which they are not like other members of the staff. These boil down, largely, to terms of employment and hours. Interns generally will be with the repository for a fixed, brief period of time. Though volunteers may be "on board" for a longer period, they are surely not there under the same status as permanent, paid staff members.

These considerations determine, to a large extent, the management of adjunct personnel. How much training is a manager willing to give an intern who will only be available for a few months? How much responsibility should be entrusted to a volunteer who is only available on an irregular basis? Managers need to ensure that volunteers and interns result in a "profit" to the institution, that is, that the investment in their training does not exceed

A volunteer retrieves material for a user. *(John R. Kennedy, courtesy Westchester County New York Archives)*

the benefit the institution derives from their presence.

In dealing with interns, managers need to ensure that the terms of the internship, as agreed upon with the sponsoring school or other institution, are followed. If the internship will result in course credit or some other benefit, the intern's performance needs to be monitored so that the institution can attest to the completion of the internship.

While volunteers can be a wonderful resource, they can also test a manager's skill. Volunteers gain a measure of independence from their status that only a foolish manager would overlook. While recognizing that volunteers may be exempt from some rules that apply to the permanent staff, management needs to make clear which apply to one and all. For instance, volunteers should be expected to work the hours for which they are scheduled.

Managing Your Peers, Managing the Boss

Managers, especially those working in large, hierarchically complex organizations will find themselves dealing with other managers at their same level. Every manager also deals with a higher authority, whether a superior manager, a board of trustees, or advisors. How does the manager handle these relationships?

One way of dealing with peers is to see them as rivals for resources and personal advancement. There is no way to eliminate the competitive aspect of peer relationships, but competition can take the form of an ordered process or it can deteriorate into a war "of all against all." No sane person should wish for such destructive behavior, but it happens, and when it does, everyone involved looks petty and ridiculous in the eyes of subordinates and superiors alike.

As in most managerial contexts, good communication is essential. Though some organizations (and some insecure executives) discourage direct lateral communication between departments, most now encourage it. "Team building" has become an important term in managerial training, and many organizations treat it as far more than a mere slogan.

In matters affecting cooperation between subordinate elements of an organization, the principle that what is not forbidden is permitted should apply. If the heads of two branches or departments agree to work on something in a way that is not forbidden by policy (for example, the cross-training of personnel assigned to the departments), they should not be required to ask for permission. It would be appropriate for the department heads to inform higher authority of the project, ask for suggestions, and promise to provide information on results. The worst that can happen is that higher authority will inform the department heads involved that it works on the alternate premise: "What is not expressly permitted is forbidden."

"Managing the boss" should not be a euphemism for toadyism. One of a manager's prime responsibilities, however, is to use allotted resources to meet a portion of the organization's objectives. Upper management is entitled to—and in most cases will require—feedback from subordinate managers on how each part of the overall effort is going. Managers should take pains to see that this response is provided in the form required by the organization and in a manner that least imposes on higher management's time and attention. Longer, more formal reports, such as an annual review, should be preceded by an executive summary, no more than two pages in length, highlighting key objectives, accomplishments, shortfalls, and plans to redress those shortfalls. Where senior management has identified major organizational goals and objectives, reports should focus on the archives' achievements in meeting them.

Most archival managers will find themselves lacking personnel, space, equipment, or money to achieve their goals. Upper management should know what shortages are preventing full accomplishment of the archives' plan; archival managers must recognize that every department is likely to be bombarding the boss with similar complaints. The subordinate manager's job is to make sure that upper management knows what shortages exist and understands the consequences of those shortages. The subordinate manager then must do the best job possible with the resources available.

People: The Central Resource

By now it should be clear that management is at least as much art or craft as science. Henry Mintzberg, a leading expert in management theory, has concluded that the "management processes are enormously complex and mysterious . . . drawing on the vaguest of information and using the least articulated of mental processes." In no area is this more true than in managing people, because in no other area does the manager have to confront more directly the realities of what kind of person he or she is and how he or she deals with other people. No amount of managerial training can make the naturally shy, aloof person a center of warmth. Moreover, there are compelling reasons—practical as well as ethical—to argue that no management training program has the right to try. Ultimately, schemes that attempt to impose changes in attitude, behavior, and even personality on managers are less likely to be successful than those which aim for the less ambitious goal of helping managers identify their inclinations and interests. Self-awareness is almost certainly more important than adapting to a preconceived mold.

Personnel management, at least on the scale likely to be practiced by most archival managers, involves direct and potentially uncomfortable contact with other persons. These contacts can be frustrating and even painful; they can also be exciting and rewarding. Success in these dealings can be critical to the success of the organization for which a manager has accepted responsibility. How management treats people can define the whole character of an organization, which is not surprising if one accepts the view of management expert Tom Peters that "organizations are collections of human beings—period." No manager can afford to be indifferent to the task of directing the human resource.

Suggested Readings

Any number of introductory personnel management textbooks are on the market, among them Dale S. Beach, *Personnel.* 5th ed. (New York: Macmillan, 1985). Raelin's *Clash of Cultures* (cited in Suggested Readings after Chapter 1) provides useful information on managing "salaried professionals." One useful approach to identifying the personality characteristics people—managers or not—bring to the job is the Myers-Briggs Type Indicator. See Sandra Krebs Hirsh, *Using the Myers-Briggs Type Indicator in Organizations: A Resource Book* (Palo Alto: Consulting Psychologists Press, 1985).

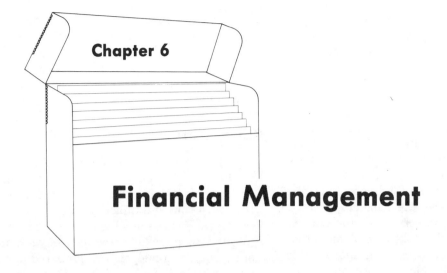

Chapter 6

Financial Management

Whatever the size of a repository, it consumes resources, both material and human.[1] It needs to account for the resources it uses and to plan for the acquisition of the resources needed to continue its operations into the future. Beyond accounting and planning for operations at the current level, financial management is critical to any effort to expand, grow, or perhaps even escape from the archival "cycle of poverty."

Organizations normally account for their income and expenses to three major audiences: external regulatory or legal authority, higher management within the organization's parent institution, and the managers of the organization itself. Each has its own uses for financial management data, and these dictate the form accountability must take.

External authorities can include the Internal Revenue Service and other governmental bodies, as well as foundations and endowments which normally require financial statements in return for grants or other funds. Whether the management of a repository reports to higher authority within a parent institution or to a board of trustees, such authorities require evidence that the staff of the repository is carrying out its responsibilities in accordance with approved policies. Finally, managers within the repository need accurate financial information to document performance, to make the best use of limited resources, and to indicate trends in operations that may require their attention.

Understanding the Financial Environment

As in every other aspect of management, finance requires a careful review and understanding of an organization's operating environment. How does the repository acquire the money with which it operates? What are the sources of that money, and what procedures are involved in obtaining it? On the other side of the ledger are expenses. How does the organization expend the resources allocated to it? What authorities must grant permission before the organization commits resources to equipment, personnel, facilities, or other costs? What requirements does the allocating authority impose for accounting for the use of those revenues?

The answers to these questions represent the financial control function of management; finance is equally important in the planning function. Will the demands on a repository's staff or facility grow over the next three years? Five years? If so, will the repository be in a position to deal with these increases by adding personnel, enlarging facilities, or otherwise expanding? Or will it be forced to retrench, to turn away collections because of lack of space, or to handle its materials poorly because of inadequate staff? Financial planning is essential in mapping out the real costs of change over time and for alerting management (within the repository), resource allocators, and possibly other constituent groups (researchers) of the repository's efforts to cope with change. Finan-

---

[1] The authors will focus principally on the financial obligations of relatively small repositories, i.e., those which do not have a professional budget and accounting staff, and whose operations do not require capital budgets and other instruments used by large institutions.

cial management, like other management functions, operates within a perpetual cycle, with plans and operations being adapted as required by changing circumstances.

Financial Planning

Managers must fully integrate financial planning with plans for the acquisition and use of personnel, facilities, and other resources.[2] (See Chapter 4 for a more thorough discussion of the planning process.) Once an organization has established its objectives for the period covered by the master or strategic plan, it must answer an important financial question: How much money will it take to implement that plan? Identifying this figure, even in approximate terms, is essential for the planner. An unrealistic project is best stopped before money, time, and effort are wasted and before it becomes a sacred cow with a vested right to survive. On the other hand, virtually nothing is lost by calculating the costs of projects for which funding is uncertain; in the event of an unexpected windfall, the organization should at least have a general idea of its objectives. A "wish list" can be useful in convincing resource allocators that the repository's management is actively thinking about the future; creating such a list costs very little.

The plan—and its attendant costs—must then be matched against the revenues *likely to be available* to the organization. At this point the manager may find it desirable to make two or three projections about revenue: an optimistic one, a pessimistic one, and an intermediate one. Note the absence of the designation "realistic." All revenue projections, even the extremes, should be realistic in that they reflect possibilities that might actually occur. For example, an organization applying for grant money to accomplish a project is realistic in calculating the availability of the requested funds in its optimistic forecast, especially if it has successfully competed for grants in the past. Simply hoping that some unknown benefactor will appear is not realistic.

Fiscal resources must be prioritized. The organization must know which operations have the first claim on money coming in, which come next, and so on. In most instances, current operations—being able to sustain ongoing efforts—come first. Expansion and new projects must compete for whatever is

left. This emphasis, though it may seem to discourage innovation and experimentation, is entirely appropriate for archives, which are essentially conserving institutions. Their managers would be irresponsible in adopting financial plans that expose their operations or their holdings to risk.

Budgeting

Budgets are useful both for planning and controlling funds, as products of the planning process, and as tools by which managers control the expenditure of resources. Effective budgeting is part of a multiyear process in which planning is done several (perhaps as many as three to five) years in advance of activity, and budgets are prepared and approved in the year before activity takes place. Though changes in a plan or project may be require deviations from the budget, the manager's goal should be to limit these as much as possible.

Archives should establish a fiscal year, if one is not mandated by a parent organization. Fiscal years may start at any time and may be changed (the federal fiscal cycle now starts on October 1 and ends on September 30, after decades of following a July 1–June 30 schedule). If the practical reasons for establishing a fiscal year are not readily apparent, the IRS has provided a regulatory one: organizations claiming tax-exempt status must report their income and expenses according to an exact fiscal year.

Let us assume a fiscal year based on the calendar year, January 1–December 31. An organization's multiyear cycle of planning, budgeting, and operating for the fiscal years 1990 through 1992 might have three budgets in preparation at any one time, each going through different stages of development. (See Figure 6-1.)

Thus, during fiscal year 1990, while money planned and budgeted for in earlier years is being spent, the budget for fiscal year 1991 should be in preparation, as should plans for fiscal year 1992. The

---

[2] Archives and repositories that exist within a larger institution will have to pay particular attention to coordinating their planning—including financial planning—in accordance with the procedures and policies of the parent institution.

Figure 6-1

YEAR	JAN. 1	JULY 1	DEC. 31
1990 (current year)	Funds released	Midyear review	End-of-year accounting
1991 (budget preparation year)	Budget prepared	review	Approval
1992 (planning year)	Planning preparation	Feasibility studies and cost estimates	Review and defense

Figure 6-2   Line-Item Budget of the Sample County Historical Society Fiscal Year 1991 (January 1 thru December 31)

PREPARED: AUGUST 1990					
Income	Budgeted 1989	Actual 1989	Budgeted 1990	Estimated 1990	Budgeted 1991
Dues	$17,500	17,000	18,500	18,000	18,500
Gift Shop	600	100	500	200	500
Donations	1,300	1,400	1,500	1,600	4,500
TOTAL	19,400	18,500	20,500	19,800	23,000
Expenses	Budgeted 1989	Actual 1989	Budgeted 1990	Estimated 1990	Budgeted 1991
Salaries:					
Director (p/t)	$8,500	8,500	8,700	8,700	9,000
Assistant (p/t)	3,700	3,700	3,900	3,900	4,100
Employee Benefits	2,000	2,200	2,400	2,400	2,500
Trustees' Expenses	400	430	500	675	550
Supplies:					
office	500	535	600	400	750
preservation	600	615	650	600	700
Equipment	150	150	1,500	1,650	1,100
Printing	350	400	450	500	600
Postage	300	325	400	475	525
Telephone	300	360	350	400	425
Subscriptions	200	180	150	150	200
Memberships	180	200	250	175	300
Professional:					
auditor	350	350	350	350	400
legal	200	200	0	0	0
Travel/Conference	1,200	1,140	300	150	1,200
	18,930	18,655	19,750	19,675	21,500

differences in the stages for the latter years reflect the fact that plans for 1991 must be narrowed more precisely as the moment comes for money to be approved and released. The exact sequence of steps will vary from institution to institution, as will the procedures involved in preparing, presenting, and defending proposals that must be approved by higher authorities, but the cyclical, continuous interaction of planning and budgeting should be universally applicable.

Though in larger organizations several budgets, especially capital and operating budgets, may be in use at any one time, most archival organizations will use only the latter. Simply stated, an operating budget is a projection, for a defined period of time, of the expenses needed to operate a program or operation and the revenues required to meet those expenses. The budget identifies in general terms sources of both. A sample budget is found in Figure 6-2.

What can be learned about Sample County's Historical Society from its budget? For one thing, it apparently occupies donated or otherwise free prop-

erty, leaving it only to pay its telephone bill. Its greatest expenditure is for the service of its two part-time employees. In 1990 and 1991 the society budgeted for relatively heavy equipment expenses (for personal computers, perhaps?). It seems to finance travel, possibly to a professional meeting, on a biennial basis.

Much of this is merely accounting information; what about planning? For the most part, this seems to be a conservative organization that produces its budget by taking last year's figures and adding a guess for inflation to produce next year's estimates. There are indications, however, of a more active approach. The figures suggest that the equipment purchases were planned and sequential. Moreover, it appears that the society has grown impatient with merely hoping for small annual increases in revenue through membership dues. The society is planning for a major increase in income from gifts and bequests—and should have a plan to achieve that goal. Without such a plan, this budget entry is likely to be nothing more than wishful thinking. Other points of interest include the absence of legal expenses (real and budgeted) after 1989. Has the society found a local attorney to volunteer legal services as needed? Or was the 1989 legal expense unusual and therefore not worthy of being figured into budgets for succeeding years?

Types of Budgets

The Sample County Historical Society budget reviewed above is an example of perhaps the most traditional of budget formats, the line-item budget. In this form, broad categories of expenditures are itemized, without linking those expenditures to the purpose or programs for which they were spent, and without explicit links to stated organizational objectives.

The line-item budget is a useful tool and likely will remain in use for a long time. It provides information on trends in expenditures (Which is rising faster, salaries or the cost of maintaining a facility?), and it is relatively simple to prepare. Nevertheless, its failure to link expenses and objectives, or expenses and accomplishments, limits its value, especially for organizations that expect or desire a significant change in their operations or their operating environment. If, for example, an organization's costs for equipment have increased only minimally over the years, successive line-item budgets would show this pattern. The decision to automate the organization's functions would almost certainly be reflected by a noticeable, if not dramatic, increase in equipment costs. The line-item format does not permit this increase to be explained or justified by information on the expected improvements to be achieved by this atypical increase in costs. By highlighting increased costs without providing a rationale for them, line-item budgeting can endanger a project rather than enhance its chances of gaining approval.

One solution to this problem was the development of program budgeting, in which salaries, materials, equipment, and, where applicable, building construction or maintenance are not consolidated for the entire organization but charged to various programs. In an archival setting, major programs might include general administration, acquisition and appraisal, collection maintenance, preservation, user services, and outreach. Though some organizations may choose to use either line-item or program budgeting exclusively, they can serve as complementary tools, each providing its own view of the organization's activities. What would a program budget for the Sample County Historical Society look like? (See Figure 6-3.)

The figures allocated to these various programs and functions should match the totals recorded in the line-item budget. For the small institution where the staff is employed in a number of duties, this may require seemingly arbitrary efforts to account for time spent on each duty, and additional effort to allocate costs. In this example, all telephone and membership expenses are accounted for centrally, while supplies, subscriptions, and equipment have been charged to specific functions. Is the more precise allocation worth the effort? Yes, *if* the information obtained provides a better—or even different—look at the organization's activities, or if it makes it easier for the organization to attract additional resources. Note, for example, that 25 percent of the limited money available to the historical society is charged to general administration. Is this too high? A definitive answer is hard to provide, but suppose one of the organization's goals is to provide more and better service to researchers. One way to achieve this would be to acquire more money for additional staff. An alternative would be to have the more highly paid director turn over more administrative duties to the less highly paid assistant, freeing up more of the director's time for user service or other professional duties. In addition to meeting management's objectives, this might be a better use of the society's talent. Thus program budgeting can reflect how operations reflect, or contradict, stated objectives.

An easy way for management to respond to pressure to cut administrative costs would be to allocate costs for telephone and other services to the functional programs of the society. How much does this reduce telephone costs? Not at all, of course. Such apparent legerdemain is not always deceptive or illegitimate. Suppose, for example, that most of the long-distance calls made by the society are in pursuit of collections. Why not allocate part of the telephone bill to acquisition and appraisal? Such valid examples aside, there is no point in denying the obvious: budgets can be manipulated to show what management wants them to show. Reallocation of costs to reflect more accurately the use of revenues is one thing; reallocating costs to give an impression of nonexistent savings is another. To say that the latter happens all the time or "everybody does it" does not resolve the issues raised by manipulative budget management.

Figure 6-3   Program Budget of the Sample County Historical Society Fiscal Year 1991 (January 1 thru December 31)

PROGRAM		BUDGETED 1990		BUDGETED 1991
GENERAL ADMINISTRATION				
Salaries and Benefits		$3,100		3,230
Supplies		300		375
Equipment		300		220
Printing		100		150
Postage		200		250
Telephone		350		425
Subscriptions		0		0
Memberships		250		300
Professional		350		400
	(25%)	4,950	(24.8%)	5,350
ACQUISITION AND APPRAISAL				
Salaries and Benefits		3,100		3,230
Supplies		100		125
Equipment		300		220
Printing		50		50
Postage		0		0
Telephone		0		0
Subscriptions		50		75
Memberships		0		0
Professional		0		0
	(18.2%)	3,600	(21.8%)	4,700
COLLECTION MAINTENANCE				
Salaries and Benefits		3,875		4,037.50
Supplies		100		125
Equipment		375		275
Printing		50		50
Postage		0		0
Telephone		0		0
Subscriptions		50		75
Memberships		0		0
Professional		0		0
	(22.5%)	4,450	(21.2%)	4,562.50
PRESERVATION				
Salaries and Benefits		2,325		2,422.50
Supplies		650		700
Equipment		225		165
Printing		50		50
Postage		0		0
Telephone		0		0
Subscriptions		50		50
Memberships		0		0
Professional		0		0
	(16.9%)	3,300	(15.8%)	3,397.50
USER SERVICES				
Salaries and Benefits		2,325		2,422.50
Supplies		75		100
Equipment		200		170
Printing		50		50
Postage		0		0
Telephone		0		0
Subscriptions		0		0
Memberships		0		0
Professional		0		0
	(13.6%)	2,650	(12.8%)	2,742.50
OUTREACH				
Salaries and Benefits		775		807.50
Supplies		25		25
Equipment		100		50
Printing		150		250
Postage		200		275
Telephone		0		0
Subscriptions		0		0
Memberships		0		0
Professional		0		0
	(6.4%)	1,250	(6.5%)	1,407.50

Figure 6-4

Project	Costs		Total	Rank
	1989	1990		
Automation	$1,800	$1,800	$ 8,000	1
Shelving	6,000	4,000	10,000	2
Furniture	3,000	0	3,000	3

Setting Priorities

Program budgeting can reflect an organization's priorities. The first priority, of course, must be for the society to continue to exist and maintain its current programs. The need to give current operations an implicit priority over new projects can present especially painful difficulties for archives, which generally exist in an environment of high, fixed costs (salaries and buildings, though "fixed" is a relative term) that cannot be easily pared to free money for new projects, and limited opportunities for revenue growth.[3] Let us nonetheless assume that, in addition, the society plans to improve or enhance its activities. As part of its overall planning process, let us further assume that three projects have been identified: automation of some office and archival functions, the acquisition of moveable shelving, and the purchase of new furniture for the research room. Each of these projects can then be described as program items and given a priority rating. (See Figure 6-4.)

What do these project figures indicate? First, that management has selected automation over shelving and furniture as its highest priority. Also that the furniture can be purchased in one fiscal year, with the shelving project paid for over two years. How many years will it take to finance the automation project? That is not apparent from the information supplied, though it will require funding after 1990, since $4,400 of its costs are not planned for either 1989 or 1990. By providing the full cost of the automation project, not just the costs to be incurred during the current budget/planning cycle, the repository has complied with the "full funding principle." This principle attempts to prevent managers from enticing resource allocators to approve what seem to be relatively inexpensive projects and

then returning to ask for the additional equipment, personnel, or other resources needed to make that which has already been purchased work. An example of a "less than full funding" approach would be for an organization to obtain money to buy a computer and only later indicate that it would perform more effectively with terminals and printers. In the case of the automation project, it seems likely that the institution foresees future purchases of additional terminals or perhaps additional software, training, or maintenance.

Setting priorities does not necessarily mean an organization will expend its funds according to its priorities—an apparent contradiction. If the automation project is funded with grant money, the organization in all probability would not be permitted to shift the money to buy furniture. But if the Sample County Office of Cultural Affairs offered $1500 to the historical society, how should this money be spent? It is unlikely that it could be used effectively for the automation project, an expenditure that seems to involve items costing $1800. Could cheaper items be obtained? Possibly, but would they meet the organization's needs, and would they be compatible with later purchases? Could peripherals, for example, a modem or printer, be omitted? Again, this might be a possibility, but management would have to take a hard look at whether the purchased equipment would still meet management's objectives. In fact, shelving and furniture could be better uses for the windfall, because each would seem to better adapt to partial acquisition and implementation.

One other factor to be considered in "violating" one's own priorities is the manager's sense of which activities are most likely to get the support of resource allocators. Using the previous example, the manager may choose to use the windfall for furniture or shelving because such items are not likely to be highly attractive to higher management. They may be essential for the preservation of the collection, the appearance of the repository, or the comfort of researchers, but they are unlikely to excite the boss. Automation might, especially if the boss has made a commitment to the modernization of the archives. In the same way, foundations and other granting agencies are far more likely to respond to an automation proposal than to one for refurbishing old facilities and equipment.

Monitoring and Accounting

Financial control implies both accounting for the expenditure of resources and monitoring opera-

---

[3] This was the plight faced by the National Archives in the early 1980s when relatively small budget cuts threatened NARS with major and painful decisions. If 70 percent of an institution's revenue is used to handle more or less fixed costs, budget cuts of even 3 or 4 percent can be serious, the remaining 30 percent of operations having to absorb a disproportionately severe cutback (from 10 to 13 percent) in their revenues.

tions. The expenditure of resources is usually reported in financial terms. The use of personnel would, for example, be translated into payment of salary, facilitating analysis and comparison. Most techniques used to monitor operations also emphasize reporting, where possible, in quantitative terms. This preference for quantitative results is understandable in theory, but difficult to achieve in practice. In the archival environment, arriving at the number of feet of records processed or disposed of in a given period is easy, but how does one put a numerical value on the quality of assistance provided to a researcher? This problem will not be solved here, but it should be noted that excessive attention to quantity is possible, even to the point of adversely affecting the quality of a repository's operations. Better to admit some doubt about the measurable amount of work accomplished than to permit the repository's work to fall victim to a fetish for numbers.

The archival manager is not be expected to be a licensed C.P.A., but some basic cost controls must be imposed, including explicit identification of which officials in an organization have the authority to dispense funds. Archival managers need to understand that they, as chief administrators of a repository, bear ultimate responsibility for funds placed under their control. In most instances, administrators act in a fiduciary capacity, with resources placed more in their trust than in their possession.

For most institutions, accounting is a relatively simple process of maintaining records of expenditures (receipts, invoices, etc.) and compiling that data periodically in a manner that permits the manager, auditors, or higher authorities to see that funds were disbursed in accordance with applicable policies and regulations and in pursuit of projects and objectives approved in the planning and budget processes.

For many institutions, *cash accounting*, familiar to everyone as the accounting procedure used with a checkbook, should be sufficient. Income is credited at the time it is received or made available for use, and costs are noted when bills are paid. A more complicated process, known as *accrual accounting*, may be required in larger repositories and in those that are part of larger operations, where accrual accounting is the norm.[4] An accrual system records income when it is earned by sales or services,

even if this precedes actual receipt of money owed. It accounts for expenses when they are incurred, even if payment takes place somewhat later. Accrual accounting distinguishes between *cash flow* and *funds flow*, a distinction most of us do not encounter handling our personal finances. Suppose an archives receives $1,000 a year for preservation supplies and early in the fiscal year orders $100 of such items. At the moment the commitment is made, the institution's funds available for preservation are reduced to $900, even though no money has changed hands. Once the supplies are received, periodic financial statements would have to show this expenditure, even if the bill is not due for payment in that period. A flow of funds has taken place, though no cash flow will occur until the bill is paid.

Organizations should attempt to estimate their expenditures over the course of the fiscal year in quarterly or semiannual intervals. Whatever the interval used, managers should review their performance at the end of each period. Is expenditure meeting, exceeding, or falling short of target? Are variances planned and justifiable or will they require reductions later in the year? The answers to questions such as these are essential pieces of management information.

Active Financial Management

As this discussion has suggested, financial management is far more complicated than simply preparing a budget and following it rigidly through an operating period. Circumstances change, and managers must be prepared to adapt to those changes. Some cost increases (overtime pay) can be controlled; others (a postal rate increase) cannot. The same uncertainty applies to revenue. In the case of the Sample County Historical Society, an increase in costs or a shortfall of revenue will require action on the part of management. Although little can be done with such items as salaries, early recognition of the problem might lead to cancellation of plans to attend a conference or perhaps to reduced spending on such items as supplies or postage.

What authority does the manager have to alter a budget, or to "reprogram funds?" Reprogramming rules and policies vary from organization to organization, so the best advice is to learn the policies of the institution. In many cases, a manager might have independent authority to reprogram within certain dollar limits without seeking approval from higher authority, with such approval required for larger amounts. Other organizations will, unfortunately,

---

[4] To confuse the issue, many organizations use a mixed cash-accrual system. For more information, see Loren A. Nikolai, *Principles of Accounting*. 2d ed. (Boston: Kent Publishing, 1986) or a similar introductory-level accounting text.

have more centralized controls that further limit or even eliminate independent reprogramming.

Financial planning and management can be a demanding and competitive arena. Texts on the subject are full of various ploys to enhance one's position, survive budget cuts, and gain the advantage over competitors. Language and metaphors drawn from sports and games (the shell game, the end run, the hidden-ball trick) and from warfare (divide and conquer) abound. Managers should expect that at some point they will come face-to-face with questions of legality and ethics. This manual can only suggest that managers need to know what is legal (meaning the regulations of a parent organization as well as civil statutes) and be alert to the ethical implications of their actions.

Effective, active financial management is an essential tool for the archival institution that hopes to survive, let alone prosper. An understanding of this tool can be a key to improving performance, planning for future needs, and impressing resource allocators with the effectiveness of the archival program. Used positively and aggressively, good financial management might even influence resource allocators to take a different view of the archivists they employ.

Suggested Readings

Inez L. Ramsey and Jackson E. Ramsey, *Library Planning and Budgeting* (New York: Franklin Watts, 1986) is an easy to use primer from a related discipline. Robert D. Vintner and Rhea K. Kish, *Budgeting for Not-for-Profit Organizations* (New York: Free Press, 1984) provides useful information on the budgeting cycle and samples of forms that should be readily adaptable by a variety of institutions.

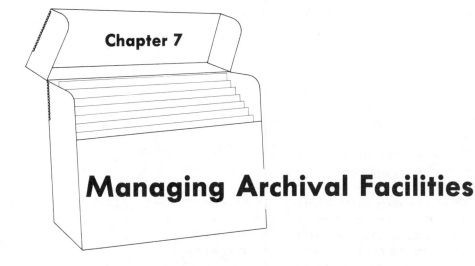

Chapter 7

Managing Archival Facilities

The word "archives" comes from the Greek word *archeion*; in English as in Greek, it refers both to the official records created by an organization and to the building or facility where they are preserved and used. Archival repositories do more than provide space for the storage of records. They also carry out other functions such as arrangement, reference, and conservation. In addition, archivists must choose equipment and supplies to furnish the archival facility. It is the responsibility of the archival administrator to secure a facility that meets minimal archival standards and that is furnished with the equipment and supplies needed to carry out fundamental archival activities. Although this chapter is directed primarily to archives with a multiperson staff, the concepts can be applied to one-person repositories with limited space.

General Facility Requirements

Regardless of the type of repository, all facilities should attempt to meet certain standards:

1. Archival repositories should maintain a constant temperature and humidity wherever records are stored or used. The optimum conditions are a temperature of sixty-five degrees Fahrenheit (plus or minus five degrees) at 50 percent relative humidity (plus or minus 5 percent). These conditions should be maintained twenty-four hours a day, 365 days per year. Repositories that cannot achieve this standard should attempt to minimize temperature and humidity fluctuations by using air conditioners, humidifiers, and dehumidifiers depending upon seasonal requirements.

2. If the archives is part of a larger building, it should be located in an area offering optimal conditions. Damp basements and dry attics should be avoided. If possible, the repository should be located away from exposed water pipes or bathrooms because of the risk of flooding and water damage.

3. Work areas should be well lighted, while light should be kept at lower levels in records storage areas. There should be as few windows as possible, and all should have curtains or blinds. Incandescent lights are preferred over fluorescent lights because they do not contain damaging ultraviolet light. All flourescent lights and outside windows should have protective UV filters.

4. All repositories should be protected against unauthorized entry and theft. Outside entrances

A hygrothermograph in use at a large archival facility measures variations in temperature and humidity. *(New York State Archives and Records Administration)*

should be minimized, and entry doors securely locked. The archivist should maintain control of all keys. An alternative to the traditional lock is access by numbered key pads or magnetic cards. Although more expensive to install, these systems can be changed more easily and less expensively than keys. An intrusion alarm should be installed; it can be supplemented by guards available for twenty-four hour duty.

5. The fire detection and suppression system will, in part, be dictated by local fire codes. A fire alarm system which can be triggered manually or automatically should be in operation twenty-four hours a day. Ionization or photoelectric smoke detectors which send an alarm automatically to a fire station or a twenty-four hour emergency service are preferred. The fire protection system may be equipped with either halon gas or dry/wet pipe water sprinklers for suppression. Sprinklers pose the danger of possible water damage to documents. The entire building should be equipped with an adequate number of fire extinguishers which use either halon or carbon dioxide. Archivists should carefully consider various alternatives available for fire suppression. Halon has been questionable as a fire suppressant because of its environmental consequences and may no longer be available from manufacturers in the future. Other factors affecting the preservation of the collection should be discussed with preservation experts.

6. Finally, repositories should be located in areas that are easily reached by the actual or potential clientele.

Components of an Archives Facility

All repositories should be organized and/or constructed to carry out archival activities: appraisal, acquisition, arrangement, description, reference, outreach, and conservation. These activities can be identified with the following building components: administration, technical services, public services, records storage, and common areas. Archival administrators must understand the archival activities and the building functions and ensure that the parent institution provides a facility to meet the repository's needs. (See Figure 7-1.)

In addition to the general needs, each functional area will have specific requirements.
- Administration
  - Entry foyer with space for a secretary-receptionist.

Figure 7-1

Building Functions

- Administration
  - Planning
  - Financial management
  - Personnel management
  - Public relations
- Technical Services
  - Acquisition
  - Appraisal
  - Arrangement
  - Description
  - Conservation
- Public Services
  - Reference services
  - Exhibits
  - Copying
  - Public programs
- Records Storage
  - Storage of all types of archival material
- Common Areas
  - Bathrooms
  - Hallways
  - Lunchroom/lounge
  - Space for utilities and equipment

- Offices with standard office equipment including desks, chairs, filing cabinets, telephones, photocopying machine, typewriters, fax modems, and/or computers.
- Storage area for office supplies.
- Technical Services
  - Areas with standard office equipment and additional work space for arrangement and description.
  - Work tables and shelving for temporary storage of records; sorting equipment.
  - Computer terminal/s for description.
  - Conservation equipment and space appropriate to the staff's abilities as well as the archives' budgetary constraints.
- Public Services
  - Welcoming, pleasant reading room with an adequate number of comfortable chairs and desks large enough to hold both records being used and the researcher's notes. It should be designed so that researchers can be monitored by either someone in the room or in adjacent offices.

- Copies of common reference material and finding aids including a computer terminal for access to data bases.
- Equipment and separate areas for using audio-visual materials.
- Space for the secure storage of coats and briefcases outside the reading room.
- An exhibit area located near the main entrance to the facility (optional).
- Conference or meeting rooms.
▸ Common Areas
- An adequate number of bathrooms for staff and researchers.
- A staff lounge or lunchroom.
- Hallways which are large enough for the adequate movement of both researchers and archival records.
▸ Records Storage
- Floors strong enough to support the shelving and records which will be placed in the facility. The necessary floor load will vary depending upon whether standard or compact, mobile shelving is used.
- Storage areas with as few doors as possible to prevent unauthorized access.
- Elevators suitable for transporting records in a multilevel stack.
- Records storage located away from possible water hazards such as pipes or bathrooms, even if this is not possible for the entire archival facility.

Functional Relationships

Each of these areas has different but equally important functions. Archivists must understand the functions, their relationships, and how the different areas interact, so that they can make the most efficient use of space and provide staff members with a facility which meets individual and institutional needs. (See Figure 7-2.)

The records storage area is integral to several repository functions. New accessions are brought from the outside entrance or loading dock to the records storage area. The staff uses the storage area to process records. Materials are brought from the records storage area to researchers in the reading room. In a large archival facility these relationships must be carefully reviewed to ensure that records can be quickly and easily brought to researchers while at the same time the storage area can be protected from unauthorized entry.

The processing area be should adjacent to the storage area so that collections can be removed for processing and then returned to storage. However, the work area must be separated by walls and/or windows from the reading room so that talking and office noise will not disturb persons carrying out research.

The placement of staff offices depends largely upon function. Staff with processing responsibility should be located close to the archives storage area but should not be directly accessible to researchers. The offices of reference personnel should be close to the storage area and the entrance, while providing direct supervision of and access to the reading room. Administrative offices should be located away from the reading room and storage areas, but close to the entrance.

The reading room should be designed so that there is only one entrance/exit, and so that people leaving the reading room pass by the office or desk of a staff member. The area should be carefully monitored whenever there is a researcher in the room. In larger facilities there may be a staff member or guard stationed in the room during the entire time it is open. Larger repositories may also have separate areas for microfilm readers or space to use typewriters, computers, or tape recorders.

Most repositories will have some common areas. Larger archives may have exhibit space, meeting rooms, or theaters. Such space should be carefully integrated into the overall facility, but should not, under normal circumstances, be directly accessible from the reading room.

Allocating Space

How much space is needed to operate an archival program? The amount of floor space, measured in square footage, needed for each of the five functions will depend upon a number of factors:

1. the size of the collection,
2. the number of staff members,
3. the number of tasks for which the archives is responsible, and
4. the number of researchers and other clients who are served.

Although there are standard measurements used in planning new buildings, the manner in which a building is organized may have a major impact on whether space can be allocated in the most efficient manner.

In planning storage space, an archival administrator can plan to store approximately 1.5 cubic feet

Figure 7-2 Functional Relationships Matrix

	Curator's Office	Director's Office	Special Projects Office (Unassigned)	Reception Area	Meeting Room/ Classroom	Kitchen	Lounge/ Lunch Room	Quiet Reading Room	Reference/ Consultation Area	Photoduplication Area & Supply Storage	Processing Workroom	Collection Storage	Preservation Laboratory
Curator's Office													
Director's Office	2												
Special Projects (Unassigned)	2	3											
Reception Area (Exhibits)	2	2	2										
Meeting Room? Classroom	3	2	3	2									
Kitchen	3	3	3	3	1								
Lounge/ Lunch Room	3	3	3	3	3	1							
Quiet Reading Room	2	3	3	2	2	3	2						
Reference/Consultation Area	1	2	2	2	2	3	2	1					
Photoduplication & Supply Storage	2	3	2	1	3	3	3	2	2				
Processing Workroom	1	3	2	3	3	3	2	3	2	1			
Collection Storage	3	3	3	3	3	3	3	2	2	3	3		
Preservation Laboratory	3	3	3	3	3	3	3	3	3	3	3	2	
Loading Dock	3	3	3	3	3	3	3	3	3	3	3	2	1

1. Immediate Adjacency Required
2. Proximity Required
3. Proximity Not Required

(Courtesy of Social Welfare History Archives, University of Minnesota)

of records for each square foot allotted to storage, assuming the use of standard shelving with aisles between each range. The use of mobile, compact shelving can nearly triple the storage capacity of records to nearly 4.5 cubic feet of records for each square foot of storage.

Standard office space should be allotted at approximately 100–125 square feet for each staff member. If the person has technical services responsibility, this amount should be increased by 50–75 percent to accommodate storage of materials being processed. This space can be arranged as individual offices or provided as a large open space with partial partitions. Open space with movable partitions offers greater flexibility while individual offices give staff members greater privacy. The amount of office space allocated to particular individuals may be adjusted upwards depending upon their responsibilities and space needs. For example, reference archivists may require additional space if they spend time in the office interviewing researchers or holding conferences with reference staff.

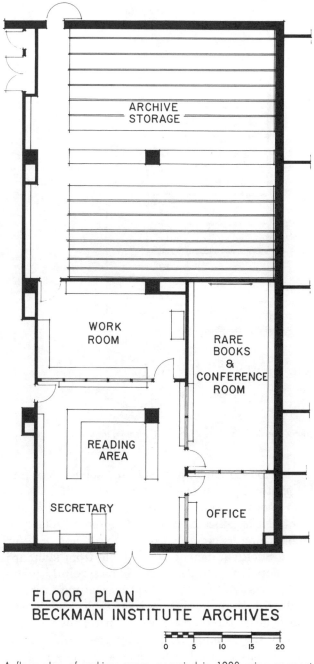

Standard fixed industrial metal shelving. *(Daughters of Charity Archives, Albany, New York)*

FLOOR PLAN
BECKMAN INSTITUTE ARCHIVES

```
0    5    10   15   20
```

A floor plan of archives space occupied in 1990 using compact shelving. *(Institute Archives, California Institute of Technology)*

Space in the reference area should average approximately 40–50 square feet for each researcher. This will include space for one desk, one chair, and a free area around the desk. In addition to this space, a certain amount of floor space must be made available for card catalogs, indexes, reference books, and other finding aids which should be in the reading room, as well as for book trucks and records in use.

Archival Equipment

In addition to space, all repositories require a minimum level of equipment to operate effectively. An archives may begin with cast-off filing cabinets, but this should not substitute for standard metal shelving. For standard paper records, 18–22 gauge metal shelving with a baked enamel finish is recommended. The archival administrator should choose shelves which are designed to hold approximately 150–200 pounds. A common arrangement for repositories using records center boxes are shelves which are fifteen inches deep, forty-two inches long, and arranged in bays six shelves high with aisles at least thirty-two inches wide. In this configuration, the metal uprights holding the shelves in place should be able to withstand a weight of 900 pounds, the average weight which can normally be stored on six shelves.

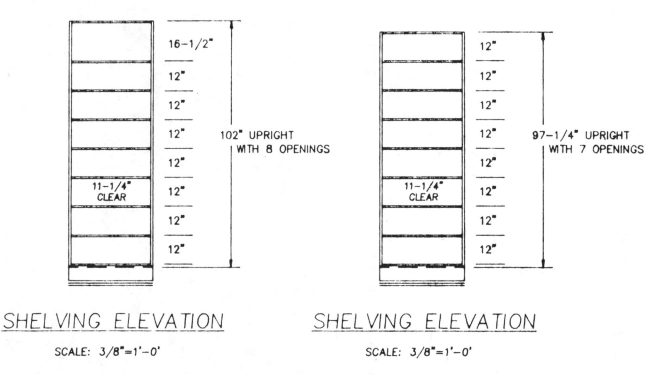

CANTILEVER SHELVING   FOUR POST RECORDS CENTER SHELVING

SHELVING ELEVATION   SHELVING ELEVATION

SCALE: 3/8"=1'-0'   SCALE: 3/8"=1'-0'

A diagram of shelving elevations for moveable cantilever and fixed records center shelving. *(Institute Archives, California Institute of Technology)*

The use of records center boxes maximizes the use of existing floor space. Although compact shelving can be used to greatly increase available space, there are space-saving alternatives for standard shelving as well. One method is the use of double-depth shelving with one box stored behind another. Double shelving eliminates one aisle but requires staff to move one box to gain access to the one behind it. It should only be erected in situations where material is not heavily used. Another alternative is high-rise shelving. Installing ranges more than six shelves high will increase shelving density by taking advantage of unused vertical space. Access to tall shelving requires a suspended catwalk or a manual or machine-supported ladder or platform.

In addition to high-density shelving, most repositories need a variety of equipment for the storage of other types of boxes and materials. Repositories with large book collections will require library shelving thirty-six inches long and nine inches deep. The repository should purchase deeper shelving for over-size volumes so that they can lie flat, thus preserving their bindings. Some filing cabinets will probably be needed for storage of actively used subject files and for photograph storage.

Repositories require a variety of office equipment: desks, office chairs, reading-room tables and seats, filing cabinets, book shelves, and similar items. Such equipment is available from standard office suppliers, but items should be carefully evaluated to ensure that they meet specialized archival needs. For example, reading-room tables should provide a large tabletop for work space; for security reasons they should be entirely open underneath with no panels or other barriers which might block a reading-room supervisor's view.

When purchasing new equipment, the archivist must choose from a variety of equipment and manufacturers. The archival administrator should begin by collecting literature and information on a variety of equipment and companies. This should be followed by discussions with sales personnel who will be able to explain the different features of their products as well as indicate expected costs. The archivist should ask for the names of institutions who have used the equipment sold by particular companies. This should

Figure 7-3

Shelving Terminology

Aisle—The amount of open space between two ranges of shelving. Aisles can vary from twenty-four to thirty-six inches in width, but must be wide enough to maneuver trucks and to load and unload boxes and volumes.

Bay—A vertical row of shelves.

Compact Shelving (also called movable or mobile shelving)—A series of shelving ranges set on platforms. The platforms sit on tracks allowing the range to be moved manually or automatically right or left. Compact shelving allows a repository to use as little as one aisle for an entire records storage area, increasing the amount of material which can be stored in a given area.

Floor Loading—The number of pounds which a floor will support, usually given in pounds per square foot. The floor load will vary depending upon the type of building construction. The greater the shelving density, the higher the required floor load. Information on floor load is generally available from building specifications. If there is any doubt, a structural engineer should be consulted.

Gauge—Term used to describe the thickness of metal shelving. The lower the number, the thicker and stronger the metal.

Library Shelving (also called cantilever shelving)—Shelving which is supported only by uprights at the rear corners of the shelf. The shelf is attached to the uprights by hooks on the shelf. The holes on the upright are one inch apart, allowing for easy height adjustment of individual shelves. Library shelving is most often used for bound volumes and manuscript boxes. It is usually thirty-six inches in length and comes in a variety of depths.

Range—One row of shelving bays.

Records Center Shelving (also called industrial shelving)—Shelving which is supported by uprights at all four corners. The shelving is usually attached to the uprights by bolts and cannot be easily adjusted for varying heights. Standard records center shelving is forty-two inches long, fifteen inches deep, and is designed to store three records center boxes per shelf. Some records center shelving is designed to hold six boxes, with one box stored behind another.

Shelving Density—The number of shelves which can be installed in a fixed amount of space. This amount can be affected by the number or width of the aisles or by the height of the shelving.

Compact shelving allows for greater utilization of space. *(Robert Paz, courtesy Institute Archives, California Institute of Technology)*

be followed up by telephone calls and on-site visits to learn about customer satisfaction and the equipment's operational effectiveness. If there is more than one company which manufactures equipment meeting institutional needs and its vendors have comparable reputations, bids should be requested so that the archival manager can choose the lowest price.

If the repository's parent agency purchases its equipment from one particular manufacturer, and the manufacturer also makes products suitable for an archival environment, the archivist may wish to go no further in seeking new equipment. If this is not the case, the archivist may wish to find several companies who manufacture a wide range of equipment and seek bids on an entire package.

Archival Supplies

Archives only periodically face the task of purchasing equipment, but they must continually buy supplies for many ongoing tasks. Supplies range from mundane items such as stationery, pencils, and pens to more specialized items including archival boxes, folders, and conservation supplies. In choosing supplies, the archival administrator must balance cost against the minimum standards needed to protect archival material. For standard office supplies which do not involve archival material, the only considerations are usefulness and price. However, where items are used in direct connection with archival material, these supplies must not harm documents and should be able to slow their deterioration.

The usefulness of different archival products should be tested by direct comparison. Manufacturers of archival supplies generally provide samples which can be compared for usefulness, quality, and archival stability. Such comparisons can also be carried out at archival meetings where suppliers often display their products. In addition, the administrative archivist should collect catalogs and manufacturers' price lists so that accurate cost comparisons are available.

Archivists must not stop at this level if they wish to ensure that the material in the archives is carefully preserved. Technical information and specifications, if not included with archival supplies, must be requested and compared with similar products available in the marketplace. Archivists can contact a reputable conservation laboratory or the Society of American Archivists for assistance.

The archivist almost always may choose from among a number of products. By carefully evaluating those choices, the repository can purchase supplies which meet its needs and which are cost-effective. Once the initial choice is made, the archivist should not assume that the repository can go on purchasing the same materials year after year with no further thought or concern. The archives must continually evaluate supplies to ensure that they meet consistent standards. Unsatisfactory supplies should be returned to the manufacturer for replacement or credit. If not satisfied, the archivist should seek an alternate supplier.

In addition, the archivist should be alert for new products or modified products that meet the repository's needs. New products may be found in announcements in professional literature or in catalogs or sales literature. Only by constant vigilance can the administrative archivist purchase the highest quality and most cost-effective products.

Reviewing Space Needs

As repositories grow, archivists make decisions about the space they occupy while evaluating the larger issues affecting the archival facility. Sometimes a new staff member's desk is added here, a computer there, and a photocopying machine somewhere else. Growth by serendipity can sometimes have unexpected effects on both employee effectiveness and the working environment, if great care is not exercised. Space can become crowded, a photo-

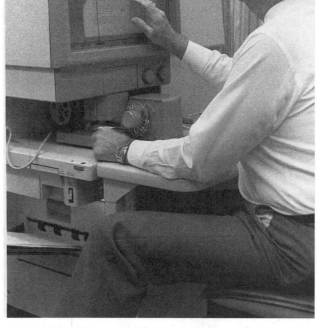

Among the equipment needed by a contemporary archives is a microfilm reader-printer. *(Gary Griffith, courtesy Louisiana Baptist Convention Archives)*

copying machine can raise the ambient temperature of the room, or the loud noise of a computer printer may interfere with telephone conversations.

Such problems should not be underestimated, and an archival administrator should constantly evaluate the facility to discover ways in which it can be more effectively used. In the same way that archivists plan an annual budget, they should frequently schedule a facility review. Is there sufficient space for the expected acquisition of archival collections during the next one-, three-, or five-year period? Do future budgets include funds for additional staff? Will there be sufficient space for these individuals? Are there plans to introduce computers? If there is space for equipment, what is the most logical placement, and what impact will it have on departmental relationships?

Answers to questions like these can often be found through research in books and publications on facilities and equipment. While archival literature

Acid-free folders and acid-free boxes are essential supplies for a contemporary archives. *(Gary Griffith, courtesy Louisiana Baptist Convention Archives)*

on such subjects is limited, a review of library and records management articles may prove extremely helpful. A thorough discussion with other staff members can also prove valuable, since their use of space and equipment provides them with insight into the relationships between the two.

If personal research and insight are insufficient, outside experts can help. One might start with other archivists who have recently reorganized or renovated buildings. Their experience and insight can be combined with visits to their facilities for tours and discussion. Most repositories are part of a larger organization which may have a property department responsible for developing new buildings or supervising renovations. Their experience can be extremely valuable in reorganizing space or planning renovations. They should be familiar with a variety of equipment and techniques to maximize space and plan for the relationships between different parts of the archives.

Other resources are available. For a fee, firms that specialize in space planning can review the space available, record the functions that occur within the space, and develop a logical and effective plan. Unfortunately, few of these companies have dealt specifically with archival repositories. Certainly their personnel will be able to apply their expertise from other projects, but archivists should take special care to ensure that the recommendations meet the repository's needs.

If funds are not available, and the repository has a specific problem which involves both space and equipment, an archives can sometimes call on one or more equipment manufacturers for advice. From work and experience in other libraries and archives, such firms can provide planning expertise. For example, shelving companies can make suggestions about the types and arrangement of shelving. They might suggest the installation of compact shelving to replace already existing shelves. Such advice can be extremely helpful, but the archival administrator must always remember that it is not totally altruistic, since the company providing the advice is also seeking to sell its products.

Planning an Expanded Facility

Archivists can carefully plan and reorganize existing space, but there will be times when the repository's need for work and/or storage space has outstripped existing resources. When faced with such a dilemma, the administrative archivist must carefully develop a strategy which meets the archives' space needs. One alternative is to expand into adjacent space. Can other offices be moved to allow further expansion? Is such space suitable for archival purposes? Is expansion a politically viable solution within the structure of the parent institution? If the answer is yes to all of these questions, the archivist has found a solution to the space problems and can get on with planning for renovation and expansion.

If the answer to any of these questions is no, the archivist must seek other solutions. If storage space is the major concern, the repository can seek to compress its records storage through the use of microfilm or optical disks. This, however, is an expensive alternative and is available in only a few select cases. Another alternative is to develop off-site storage for records. This may solve short-term space needs but creates other problems of access or perhaps inadequate environmental controls. With large increases in staff or holdings, the archivist must seek

Figure 7-4

PROJECTING FUTURE STORAGE NEEDS

1. Current Volume of Records Stored: 3,100 Cubic Feet

2. Annual Increase: $\dfrac{3,100 \text{ cf}}{10 \text{ years}} = 310$ cf of annual increase

3. If the repository must plan its new facility so that it has space for an additional fifteen years it will need:

    310 cf per year

$\times$ 15 years

    4,650 additional cubic feet of storage

4. Total Storage Needs:

    3,100   cubic feet of current records storage

 +4,650   cubic feet of additional storage

    7,750   cubic feet is the total needed for the next fifteen years.

---

a different facility to meet both immediate and long-term needs.

Whether the repository is expanding into additional space or planning for a new facility, much of the planning and preparation will be the same. The administrative archivist's first step must be to evaluate the short-term and long-term space needs of the archives in conjunction with its long-range plan. What is the current number of staff members? What changes in staffing are expected in the next one, five, or ten years? A second area of concern is the expected increase in the size of the archival collection. This cannot be predicted with absolute accuracy, but statistics on annual increases in the collection can provide the parameters for future space needs. If the repository has not collected such data, annual growth can be extrapolated by dividing the total volume of the collection by the number of years that the institution has been in existence, as in Figure 7-4.

A third concern in future planning is providing space for current and projected researchers. Such planning is facilitated by keeping accurate records of the number of researchers who visit the archives and projecting the amount of growth over a period of years. Future needs can be projected in a fashion similar to that used for storage space. When planning space requirements for researchers, the archives administrator should take into account not only the reading room but also the space required for additional bathrooms, handicapped access, areas to store coats and bags, and other needs connected with this function. Overlooking such areas leads to overcrowding of facilities, both for staff and researchers.

A fourth concern should be the security of the collection. Current security measures should be reviewed. Even if they have been adequate, planning for a new facility will allow the administrative archivist to upgrade security measures and install more modern equipment. Because of the specialized nature of security systems, it may be helpful to seek the advice of a security consultant.

Finally, space plans should include current or new archival functions developed through institutional planning. These might include exhibit areas, conference rooms, lecture halls, conservation laboratories, and audio-visual use areas. Again, current and future space needs should be projected. However, such projections will be speculative in nature and hard to defend on the basis of past statistics. This task will be made easier by linking the long-range plan of the repository with building plans.

Once all the data on current and future needs has been collected, the repository can indicate to its parent organization the amount of additional space which must be added to its current facility or the total amount needed in a new or different building. Negotiating for new space is a political process requiring both skill and nerve. In making a presentation, the archivist must strongly support needs for space. Such a stance is made easier if there is factual and statistical evidence which supports its needs. Archivists should never fear asking for the resources needed to do their work, and space is one of those commodities which an archives needs to function.

If the building concept is approved, the administrative archivist must discuss alternative means of financing the facility. Will funds be allocated by the parent institution, or will money be raised from donors or private foundations? Such decisions are usually out of the archivist's hands, but in some cases may become the archivist's responsibility.

Working with Architects and Contractors

Once the parent institution approves the release of space needed for expansion or construction of a new facility, the archives administrator becomes involved in an odyssey of education and frustration. Almost immediately the archivist will be thrust into a world of construction terms, blueprints, and building personnel who have little or no knowledge of what an archives is or does. The archivist's ability to learn quickly, to communicate effectively, and to educate architects and builders working on the building may mean the difference between a carefully constructed, fully functional facility and one which requires significant changes or operational compromise once it is completed.

One of the first tasks which the archivist confronts is the selection of an architect. In most cases the archivist will have little or no choice in this matter. Some organizations have an architect with whom they normally work and are unwilling or unable to seek other choices. Others operate on a bidding system and select the lowest bidder. While there are advantages to using an architect who is familiar with an institution's buildings and personnel, if there is a choice, the archivist should seek an architect experienced in the specialized needs of an archives or research library. If the archivist does play a role in selecting the architect, every effort should be made to visit buildings designed by the architect and talk with persons occupying those facilities. Using an architect who already has a working knowledge of archival and library functions will, in the long run, save the archivist time and energy and should result in a more functional building. If archivists are involved in negotiations of the architect's contract, they should understand exactly what the architect has agreed to do. The primary contract will call for designing the building or space within a larger facility, but the architect can also be asked to:

1. Do a program study to evaluate the amount of space needed for different building functions.
2. Do a site comparison and analysis between two or more possible locations for a new archival facility.
3. Select additional equipment such as furniture or shelving.

Such items should be discussed and responsibilities assigned before agreeing to a contract.

If the architect has not worked on an archival facility, the archivist must begin an educational program explaining various archival functions, how they relate to one another, and the amount of space needed to carry them out. At an early stage the administrative archivist should create a list of functional areas that must be included in the new building and the amount of space needed for each. The list should be accompanied by a program statement outlining archival activities and their relationships which can be used to educate both architects and contractors. At the same time, the architect should outline relevants building and fire codes which affect both renovations and new construction and how these may affect the archival facility.

If the preliminary planning has been thorough, this process should go smoothly and quickly. In designing the building, the architect will combine this information with other factors such as cost, volume of space, and design to come up with a final plan. During the design phase, the architect will present three successive sets of drawings and blueprints. At each stage the archivist must carefully review these documents and suggest changes or corrections. The archivist should not be afraid to ask the architect questions. Archivists who are unfamiliar with blueprints or who have little experience with planning buildings should call upon their institution's property department, members of the repository staff, friends, or colleagues to go over the plans for comments and suggestions. They may also want to consider hiring a consultant with experience in reviewing library or archival facilities. Archivists can educate themselves through reading and research. One book which may be helpful is the *Dictionary of Architecture and Construction* by Cyril Harris. (See Suggested Readings at the end of this chapter.)

Changes in the plans are fairly easy to make during the early planning stages. However, as time passes it becomes increasingly difficult, if not impossible, to make changes, so it is incumbent upon the archivist to carefully review the plans before they become finalized and construction begins. Great care must be taken in evaluating the location of functional archival areas, the placement and size of doors and windows, the width of aisles, and similar details. Although it is impossible to foresee how a facility will operate while it is only in the blueprint stage, the archivist must make a careful and considered attempt to ensure that it meets the institution's needs.

Building Construction

The building plans go through several stages until the final plan is accepted. After the plan is complete, the institution may call upon the contractor it normally uses to give a cost estimate or ask for bids from a number of firms. The bidding process will reflect the architect's plans including specifications for such things as heating, air conditioning and climate control, fire protection, and security systems.

If the repository has dealt with subcontractors for specific services such as climate control or fire protection, it can request that such vendors be used by the contractor who is making the bid. Where the archives has no previous contact with such special-

The final letter is swung into place for a new archival facility. *(T. C. Fitzgerald, courtesy Archives, Commonwealth of Massachusetts)*

ists, it can seek recommendations and suggestions from other archivists or from conservation laboratories or consultants. Such efforts must be completed before the bidding takes place so that the subcontractor's costs can be included. If there is more than one bid, the institution must compare the bids based upon cost as well as the reputation of the firms when selecting a contractor.

The archivist's work is not done once construction begins. The archivist should visit the site on a regular basis to check progress and compare the blueprints with the actual construction. The archivist should keep in close contact with the contractor since there will still be some decisions to make, particularly if construction falls behind schedule or the contractor discovers major difficulties in meeting the specifications given in the plans.

The result of all of these efforts should be a new or remodeled building which is efficiently designed and will meet the needs of the repository for many years to come. Such is the result of careful planning by the archivist, the involvement of a creative architect, and the work of skilled craftsmen.

Even with a nearly-completed reading room in a new facility, an archivist must closely follow progress right to the end. *(Robert Paz, courtesy Institute Archives, California Institute of Technology)*

Conclusion

While not every archivist will build or remodel an archival facility, all archivists are faced with planning for the best use of their facilities as well as for the purchase of supplies and equipment. Such decisions have a significant impact on the total program and should always be carefully considered. Through applied common sense backed by thorough research and information gleaned from conservation experts, the archivist should be able to make decisions which lead to positive results and an improved archival program.

Suggested Readings

There is a dearth of archival literature on the organization and planning of archival facilities. The most detailed information can be found in Ann Pederson, *Keeping Archives* (Sydney, Australia: Australian Society of Archivists, 1987), pp. 39–62. Although somewhat out of date, the following is a useful volume: Timothy Walch, *Archives and Manuscripts: Security* (Chicago: Society of American Archivists, 1977).

Archivists planning new facilities should review publications prepared by related professions. Two publications from the museum world are Catherine R. Brown et al., *Building for the Arts: A Guidebook for the Planning and Design of Cultural Facilities* (Washington, D.C.: American Association of Museums, 1984); and Suzanne Stephens, ed., *Building The New Museum* (Washington, D.C.: American Association of Museums, 1986). Some general publications include Philip D. Leighton and David C. Weber, *Planning Academic and Research Library Buildings* (Chicago: American Library Association, 1986); R.L. Brauer, *Facilities Planning* (New York: American Management Associations, 1986); and Cyril Harris, *Dictionary of Architecture and Construction* (New York: McGraw-Hill, 1975).

Archivists considering the purchase of supplies should carefully review Ontario Museum Association and Toronto Area Archivists' Group, *Museum and Archival Supplies Handbook* (Toronto, Ontario: Museum Association and Toronto Area Archivists' Group, 1985). The handbook lists a variety of archival suppliers and gives advice on ordering. Concerns about the quality of archival supplies are addressed in the Society of American Archivists' manuals on conservation and photographs: Mary Lynn Ritzenthaler, *Preserving Archives and Manuscripts* (Chicago: Society of American Archivists, forthcoming), and Mary Lynn Ritzenthaler et al., *Archives and Manuscripts: Administration of Photographic Collections* (Chicago: Society of American Archivists, 1984).

Chapter 8

Fund Raising and Development

To achieve its goals a repository requires funding for staff, equipment, and facilities. The majority of this support should come from the budget allocation of the parent institution since it authorized the archival program and receives the greatest benefit. Sometimes, however, archival administrators may seek additional funds for building or equipping a new or renovated facility, purchasing important collections, or completing specific short-term projects requiring additional staff, equipment, or supplies. This chapter will cover such issues as financial planning, seeking internal and external resources, and planning and managing grant proposals.

Financial Planning

Fund-raising efforts grow naturally out of a repository's long-range planning. Only when the archives has clearly defined its mission, goals, and objectives should it consider seeking additional sources of support. The archival administrator must then set priorities for objectives and activities for current and future years. When completed, planning yields a list of items for which funds are available and identifies those which cannot be accomplished at current budget levels.

Before approaching institutional resource allocators or a potential funding agency, the archival administrator should carefully review the project or program that requires additional support. This review should highlight and specify:

Goals—What are the goals of the program? Is the intent to make archival collections more readily available? Is the program geared toward the conservation of collections? Is a new or remodeled facility required? Such issues should be carefully thought out before proceeding further.

Activities—Based on the stated goals, what activities will be required to achieve those goals? This profile should include not only the specific steps needed to complete the program, but also a listing of personnel, equipment, space needs, and supplies.

Costs—When the activities have been defined, the archival administrator should develop a rough estimate of the costs for the total project. This should not be an attempt to develop a finalized budget but only a general estimate of the funds that are needed. With this information the archival administrator can decide whether the project may be too large or too small for specific funding agencies.

At this point archival administrators have several choices. They can return to the administration of their parent institution to advocate the need for additional funding or immediately seek outside support. The former strategy is often successful and should be attempted before other funds are sought. Arguing for increased internal support is useful since it educates resource allocators to the needs and priorities of the archives.

Seeking Internal Funding

Archival administrators seeking funding for new programs should begin the search within their own institution before looking outward. Preparing a budget proposal requires careful planning as well as a marshalling of support. Archival administrators must familiarize themselves with available alternatives within the institution and match needs with funds. The archivist must be aware of the parent institution's budgetary structure. If funds are not available from the current operating budget, other sources might be sought. For example, some institutions retain capital reserves for constructing and remodeling facilities and purchasing capital equipment. Such reserves could be tapped for building renovations or the purchase of a new computer. Other institutions maintain discretionary and endowment funds. Some funds may be released with the approval of the parent institution's administration, others may be used only for specific purposes. Knowing the nature of these funds can be a valuable tool in seeking financial support.

The archival administrator must marshall support from internal constituencies. Two groups with a vested interest in the repository are its donors and members of its advisory committee. Chapter 9 will discuss the need for archival administrators to encourage support for the archives from different constituencies. Such support is an important ingredient in the success of every repository, but becomes critical when the archives has financial needs beyond its normal budget.

Seeking External Funding

Occasionally important programs require support for which internal funding is not available. At such times, the archival administrator must look beyond the parent institution for financial support. If the repository is part of a larger institution such as a university, a library, or a religious or charitable organization, the archivist should begin by meeting with the fund-raising or development officer. The archival administrator can gain useful insights from the development officer's expertise and learn of possible sources of financial support. The archivist will also discover if there are any restrictions on fund raising imposed by the parent institution. Some institutions require that all grants go through the development office, while others, such as religious agencies, may be unwilling to accept federal grants. If the parent institution does not have a development or fund-raising office, these issues should be dis-

cussed and cleared with the office responsible for seeking or receiving such outside funds. Whether or not the archives must channel requests through the development office, it should seek its assistance in reviewing grant proposals. Content, format, budget, and work plans should be examined. The development officer's experience can be crucial in presenting a proposal which meets the needs and timetable of a particular funding agency.

As archival administrators begin to seek outside funding, they will become acquainted with grant officers and foundation administrators. Such individuals can provide helpful advice on sources of support when a proposal falls outside an agency's guidelines. The suggestions of grant officers can also assist applicants in revising or rethinking a proposal in its nascent stages. Archival administrators should be aware, however, that fund raising is a competitive field and that their initial ideas or concepts may require considerable revision before they find someone interested in funding their project. Both repository supporters and funding agency officials should be cultivated continually. Developing a network of contacts will provide informal responses to fund-raising ideas and offer leads to other sources of support.

Capital and Endowment Campaigns

Archival administrators are often called upon to raise money for buildings or an endowment, particularly when the parent institution is unable to provide full funding. Other activities which may require outside funding are building renovations, new facilities, or ongoing programs. Once the planning exercise is complete, and both program and funding needs are clear, the archival administrator should attempt to discover whether it is possible to raise the amount of money that is required. Large fundraising projects often require additional expertise or support, and will undoubtedly involve the parent institution's development department and/or private companies or consultants who specialize in outside fund raising.

The archives should do considerable research before engaging a fund-raising firm. It should seek the names of companies from other agencies who have carried out building or endowment campaigns. It should discover the services offered and the fees charged, and obtain the names of similar organizations that have used the firm's services for references. Fund-raising companies provide a range of support from advice to full responsibility for the complete campaign. Fees for their services will vary depending upon their involvement in the campaign and may range from a set fee to a percentage of the total funds raised.

Many companies begin by carrying out a feasibility study to discover if there are sources from which to raise the needed funds. Through research, companies can pinpoint sources of financial support and indicate the level of giving. Such a study may indicate the possibility of success or require a revision of the funding goals and the resulting program.

Capital and endowment fund raising is both difficult and time-consuming. Such projects should not be embarked upon lightly and should only begin after archival administrators have the total involvement and support of the parent institution, the archives' governing board, and the parent institution's development office.

Foundations

Philanthropic giving, channeled through corporate and private foundations, provides millions of dollars each year in the form of grants to nonprofit and charitable organizations. Although foundations may seem to be the first place to seek funds, foundations should be approached only after thorough investigation by archival administrators. Foundations usually support specific types of programs and may restrict support to specific geographic locations. Some foundations may only give funds for medical research in the state of Delaware, while others limit their giving to educational programs in Milwaukee, Wisconsin. Such restrictions may be part of the guidelines originally established by the donor or may reflect the current policy of the foundation's board. Some large foundations change their program emphases over time to reflect current social needs or the board's composition or outlook.

Archival administrators should begin their search for outside funds by reviewing first the foundations in their local community and those located within their state. Starting locally or regionally, the archival administrator has a better chance of finding a foundation which might support a specific project. There are large foundations that fund library and historical projects on a national basis, but they are few in number and there is a great deal of competition for their funds.

The Foundation Center publishes *The Foundation Directory,* a list of foundations organized first by state and then alphabetically by name. Indexes include a state list, subdivided by city, and a subject index. Each listing provides financial data, purpose and activities, application information, address, and telephone number. Archival administrators should know the foundation's general giving pattern but should also discover the types of projects it has funded in recent years and the average size of grants awarded. This information is found in a data base and computer printouts compiled by the Foundation Center library. The data base can be searched for specific geographic areas or types of recipients such as libraries, archives, and historical programs. Such material can be used, without cost, at the Foundation Center library, its branches, or through major regional libraries. They also provide many services to individual institutions on a fee basis. Copies of foundation annual reports also give such data and are available at the Foundation Center library or directly from the individual foundation.

When a foundation has been identified as a possible supporter of archival programs, the administrator should approach the foundation to discover its interest in providing support for specific programs. The chance of success is improved, however, if the initial contact can be made by an archives advisory board member, an archives supporter, or someone in the parent institution's development office who is acquainted with the foundation staff or board. If this is not the case, the archival administrator should call or write the foundation. The proposal should be discussed in general terms and guidelines and applications requested. If interest is shown by the foundation, the archival administrator should begin establishing a relationship with the foundation staff and preparing a formal proposal.

Government Agencies

Some government agencies provide support for archives, libraries, and museums. Here again, the search for a likely funding source should begin at the local level and expand outward. A number of states have developed grant programs in the arts, history, or the humanities. Some state archival agencies have begun offering grants to local archival programs with funding from either federal or state sources. Archival administrators should discover whether such agencies exist in their state, the types of programs eligible for funding, and the average size of grant awards.

The federal government offers a number of grant programs of interest to archival administrators. Some of the agencies providing grants include the National Historical Publications and Records

Figure 8-1

Federal Agencies Offering Grant Support

Department of Education
555 New Jersey Avenue, N.W., Room 404
Washington, D.C. 20208-5571
(202) 219-1315

Institute of Museum Services
1100 Pennsylvania Avenue N.W., Room 609
Washington, D.C. 20506
(202) 786-0539

National Endowment for the Arts
1100 Pennsylvania Avenue, Room 624
Washington, D.C. 20506
(202) 682-5442

National Endowment for the Humanities
1100 Pennsylvania Avenue
Washington, D.C. 20506
(202) 786-0570

National Historical Publications and Records
   Commission
National Archives and Records Administration
Washington, D.C. 20408
(202) 501-5610

National Science Foundation
1800 G Street, N.W.
Washington, D.C. 20550
(202) 357-7075

Commission, the National Endowment for the Humanities, the National Endowment for the Arts, the Department of Education, the Institute of Museum Services, and the National Science Foundation. Programs range from general operating support from the Institute of Museum Services, to preservation grants from the National Endowment for the Humanities, to funds for developing inter-institutional documentation strategies from the National Historical Publications and Records Commission. (See Figure 8-1.)

The purposes of government grant programs are defined by law. There are, however, changes in emphasis over time. A review of federal agencies will indicate whether a specific federal program provides funds for the type of program planned by the repository. If this appears to be the case, the archival administrator should write to the grant agency requesting additional information on grant programs and lists of grants which have been recently awarded. A follow-up call to discuss the proposal

with a program officer is also advisable at this stage, and continued contacts are helpful at various stages of the grant-writing process.

Grant Applications

Archival administrators should learn all they can about the funding agencies to which they are applying. They should request copies of application forms, guidelines, and instructions and continue to review these during the application process to ensure that all of the funding agency's requirements are met. It may even be useful to develop a checklist of both tasks and deadlines which must be met in connection with the proposal. Applications should be concise, realistic, and tailored to the purposes of the funding agency to which they are being sent. Archival administrators must know their audience. For example, if an agency does not normally provide funds to archival programs, it may be necessary to provide more detailed information about archival procedures or goals, either verbally or through the written application. Applicants should seek advice and response from the foundation or agency before and during the application process. If it is possible to visit and meet staff members, the archivist should do so. Some government agencies hold office hours at professional meetings such as the annual meeting of the Society of American Archivists, offering an informal opportunity to discuss grant concepts or proposals in draft form. Applicants should not overlook archival colleagues as sources of information. Opinions should be sought about possible grant concepts. Finally, when an application has been drafted, a critical review by several professionals outside the repository can greatly improve a proposal. An outsider's perspective can reveal a lack of information, clarity, or logic.

Applications vary depending upon whether the repository is applying to a private foundation or a public agency. Some private foundations have a formal application form, while others ask only for a letter describing the project and the amount of money requested. In either event, applications to private foundations are likely to be shorter and require less time to complete since foundations tend to operate more informally than government agencies. Private foundations usually meet on a regular basis to review applications. Most meet quarterly, with larger ones meeting monthly and smaller ones sometimes meeting only annually or semiannually. Archival administrators should schedule their work to meet application deadlines and response dates.

The government grant application process tends to be considerably more complicated. Applications generally require much more information and are more lengthy than those of private foundations. Each agency has a specific format and requires certain types of information. Because of the time required, it is wise to discuss planned projects with agency staff before drafting a full application. Such discussion could indicate whether a proposal is competitive with other applications, or whether major changes should be made in the initial proposal. Grant staff may also be willing to review a proposal before submission, suggesting changes that will help it meet grant agency guidelines as well as make the project more effective.

Applicants must be realistic in drafting their proposals. Credibility is an important commodity with granting agencies, and repositories should not promise more than they are capable of producing. Application forms vary from agency to agency, but each should include the following types of information:

Purpose—The proposal must establish why the project is important and explain the benefits it will bring to the institution, its constituents/users, or to the archival community. This is one of the most critical issues which the proposal will address. The archival administrator must make a good case for the project, indicating not only why it is important to the institution's development, but also how it fits into a larger archival context.

Goals—The proposal must indicate what goals and objectives the institution plans to achieve in the course of the planned project. The goals and objectives should be part of the archives' larger planning process and will become a factor in the grant agency's evaluation of the grant proposal.

Plan of Work and Timetable—To reach the project's goals, the proposal should list the tasks to be completed. A schedule should indicate completion dates for various tasks. If the proposal sets targets for the amount of material processed, surveyed, or appraised, it should provide evidence that these goals can be achieved based on institutional evidence or experience at other archival institutions.

Staff—The proposal should list all staff connected with the project, indicating the role they will play in achieving project goals. The application should also include a resume or curriculum vitae for each, indicating their qualifications.

Budget—Each proposal should have a full budget listing expenses for personnel, personnel benefits, supplies, equipment, travel, or other expenses connected with the project. Most granting agencies will require matching funds or cost-sharing, and figures should be included for personnel, overhead, and indirect costs not paid by the grant. (See Figure 8-3 for a sample grant budget from the National Historical Publications and Records Commission.)

Managing Grants

The receipt of a grant is the beginning, not the end of the grant process. Too often, archival administrators are not prepared to manage the grants once they have been received. Grants require a management process which parallels that of the full archival institution. This may entail the recruitment, selection, and supervision of additional staff, maintenance of budgets, and preparation of periodic reports. There must be sufficient time allotted for archival administrators and repository staff to carry out these tasks if the grant program is to be successful.

Archival administrators should carefully review reporting guidelines. Government grants require frequent written and financial reports, while foundations generally have fewer reporting guidelines. Weekly logs or reports of completed work will ease this task. Grant funds should be segregated in a separate account for ease of reporting. With a separate fund, it will be easier to track expenditures in different categories. Some agencies allow grant funds to be placed in interest-bearing accounts, while others do not. Guidelines on these matters should be carefully followed.

Recruitment of staff should follow the procedures outlined in the grant proposal. Government granting agencies may require a national search, while foundations may have no guidelines at all. Recruiting staff may be difficult because grant projects generally are completed within one or two years. This situation can be alleviated, however, if the salary level for grant personnel is at or above permanent staff levels. Grant personnel should become an

Figure 8-3

BUDGET FORM

Project Director	If this is a revised budget, indicate the NHPRC application/grant number:
T. Woods Mann	
Applicant Organization	**Requested Grant Period**
Emerald City Government	From __4/1/90__ to __3/31/91__ mo/yr mo/yr

The three-column budget has been developed for the convenience of those applicants who wish to identify the project costs that will be charged to Commission funds and those that will be cost shared. In accordance with Federal regulations, the only column that applicants are required to complete is Column C, although applicants may wish to complete Columns A & B in order to provide sufficient detail to allow for a better understanding of their budget request. The method of cost computation should clearly indicate how the total charge for each budget item was determined. If more space is needed for any budget category, please follow the budget format on a separate sheet of paper.

When the requested grant period is eighteen months or longer, separate budgets for each twelve-month period of the project must be developed on duplicated copies of the budget form.

SECTION A—budget detail for the period from __4/1/90__ to __3/31/91__
mo/yr   mo/yr

1. Salaries and Wages

Provide the names and titles of principal project personnel. For support staff, include the title of each position and indicate in brackets the number of persons who will be employed in that capacity. For persons employed on an academic year basis, list separately any salary charge for work done outside the academic year.

name/title of position	no.	method of cost computation (see sample)	NHPRC Funds (a)	Cost Sharing (b)	Total (c)
T. Woods Mann, Project Director	[1]	12 months x 25% @ $28,000 per year	$ _____	$ 7,000	$ 7,000
Archivist	[1]	12 months x 100% @ $22,000	$ 22,000	$ _____	$ 22,000
Archives Technician	[1]	12 months x 100% @ $16,000	$ 8,000	$ 8,000	$ 16,000
_____	[ ]	_____	$ _____	$ _____	$ _____
_____	[ ]	_____	$ _____	$ _____	$ _____
_____	[ ]	_____	$ _____	$ _____	$ _____
		SUBTOTAL	$ 30,000	$ 15,000	$ 45,000

2. Fringe Benefits

If more than one rate is used, list each rate and salary base.

rate		salary base	(a)	(b)	(c)
15 %	of	$ 45,000	$ 4,500	$ 2,250	$ 6,750
_____ %	of	$ _____	$ _____	$ _____	$ _____
		SUBTOTAL	$ 4,500	$ 2,250	$ 6,750

3. Consultant Fees

Include payments for professional and technical consultants and honoraria.

name or type of consultant	no. of days on project	daily rate of compensation	(a)	(b)	(c)
_____	_____	$ _____	$ _____	$ _____	$ _____
_____	_____	$ _____	$ _____	$ _____	$ _____
_____	_____	$ _____	$ _____	$ _____	$ _____
		SUBTOTAL	$ _____	$ _____	$ _____

Figure 8-3 (continued)

NHPRC Budget Form   Page 2

4. Travel

For each trip indicate the number of persons traveling, the total days they will be in travel status, and the total subsistence and transportation costs for that trip. When a project will involve the travel of a number of people to a conference, institute, etc., these costs may be summarized on one line by indicating the point of origin as "various." All foreign travel must be listed separately.

item	no. of persons	total travel days	subsistence costs +	transportation costs =	NHPRC Funds (a)	Cost Sharing (b)	Total (c)
Emerald City/Nome, Alaska	[1]	[5]	$ 325	$ 340	$	$ 665	$ 665
	[ ]	[ ]	$	$	$	$	$
	[ ]	[ ]	$	$	$	$	$
	[ ]	[ ]	$	$	$	$	$
	[ ]	[ ]	$	$	$	$	$
	[ ]	[ ]	$	$	$	$	$
	[ ]	[ ]	$	$	$	$	$
				SUBTOTAL	$	$ 665	$ 665

5. Supplies and Materials

Include consumable supplies, materials to be used in the project, and items of expandable equipment, i.e., equipment items costing less than $5,000 per unit.

item	basis/method of cost computation	(a)	(b)	(c)
Microcomputer	1 @ $4,000	$	$ 4,000	$ 4,000
Computer printer	1 @ $500	$	$ 500	$ 500
Computer supplies	12 mos. @$16.66 per month	$	$ 200	$ 200
Shelving for stacks	10 units @$75 per unit	$	$ 750	$ 750
Acid-free archives boxes	2,000 @$1 each	$ 2,000	$	$ 2,000
Acid-free folders	12,000 @$100 per thousand	$ 1,200	$	$ 1,200
Office supplies	12 mos. @$25 per month	$	$ 300	$ 300
		$	$	$
		$	$	$
		$	$	$
	SUBTOTAL	$ 3,200	$ 5,750	$ 8,950

6. Services

Include the cost of duplication and printing, long distance telephone, equipment rental, postage, and other services related to project objectives that are not included under other budget categories or in the indirect cost pool.

item	basis/method of cost computation	(a)	(b)	(c)
Long-distance telephone	est. 50 toll calls @$3 each	$	$ 150	$ 150
		$	$	$
		$	$	$
		$	$	$
		$	$	$
	SUBTOTAL	$	$ 150	$ 150

Figure 8-3 (continued)

NHPRC Budget Form   Page 3

7. Other Costs

Include equipment purchases of $5,000 or more per unit, training costs and registration fees, and other items not previously listed. Please note that "miscellaneous" and "contingency" are not acceptable budget categories. Refer to the budget instructions for the restriction on the purchase of permanent equipment.

item	basis/method of cost computation	NHPRC Funds (a)	Cost Sharing (b)	Total (c)
Workshop registration	1 course @$250	$	$ 250	$ 250
		$	$	$
		$	$	$
		$	$	$
		$	$	$
		$	$	$
		$	$	$
		$	$	$
	SUBTOTAL	$	$ 250	$ 250

8. Total Direct Costs (add subtotals of items 1 through 7)

$ 37,700 $ 24,065   61,765

9. Indirect costs [This budget item applies only to institutional applicants.]

If indirect costs are included, check the appropriate box below and provide the information requested. Refer to the budget instructions for explanations of these options.

[X]   Current indirect cost rate(s) has/have been negotiated with a Federal agency. (Complete items A and B.)

[ ]   Indirect cost proposal has been submitted to a Federal agency but not yet negotiated. (Indicate the name of the agency in item A and show proposed rate(s) and base(s), and the amount(s) of indirect costs in item B.)

[ ]   Applicant chooses to use a rate not to exceed 10% of direct costs up to a maximum charge of $5,000. (Under item B, enter the proposed rate, the base against which the rate will be charged, and the computation of indirect costs or $5,000, whichever sum is less.)

A.   Department of Education   2/1/89
             name of Federal agency   date of agreement

B.

rate		base(s)	NHPRC Funds (a)	Cost Sharing (b)	Total (c)
20 %	of	$ 45,000	$	$ 9,000	$ 9,000
___ %	of	$	$	$	$

10. Total Project Costs (direct and indirect) for Budget Period

$ 37,700 $ 33,065 $ 70,765

Figure 8-3 (continued)

SECTION B—Summary Budget and Project Funding

SUMMARY BUDGET

Transfer from section A the total costs (column c) for each category of project expense. When the proposed grant period is eighteen months or longer, project expenses for each twelve-month period are to be listed separately and totaled in the last column of the summary budget. For projects that will run less than eighteen months, only the last column of the summary budget should be completed.

Budget Categories	First Year/ from: 4/1/90 to: 3/31/91	Second Year/ from: to:	Third Year from: to:		TOTAL COSTS FOR ENTIRE GRANT PERIOD
1. Salaries and Wages	$ 45,000	$	$	= $	45,000
2. Fringe Benefits	$ 6,750	$	$	= $	6,750
3. Consultant Fees	$	$	$	= $	
4. Travel	$ 665	$	$	= $	665
5. Supplies and Materials	$ 8,950	$	$	= $	8,950
6. Services	$ 150	$	$	= $	150
7. Other Costs	$ 250	$	$	= $	250
8. **Total Direct Costs (items 1-7)**	$ 61,765	$	$	= $	61,765
9. Indirect Costs	$ 9,000	$	$	= $	9,000
10. **Total Project Costs (Direct & Indirect)**	$ 70,765	$	$	= $	70,765

PROJECT FUNDING FOR THE ENTIRE GRANT PERIOD

Requested from NHPRC:[1]   Cost Sharing:[2]

Outright $ 37,700   Cash Contributions $

Matching $ In-Kind Contributions $ 33,065

                                                                           Project Income $

                                                                           Other Federal Grants[3] $

TOTAL NHPRC FUNDING $ 37,700   TOTAL COST SHARING $ 33,065

Total Project Funding (NHPRC Funds + Cost Sharing)[4] = $ 70,765

[1]Indicate the amount of outright and/or Federal matching funds that is requested from the Commission.

[2]Indicate the amount of cash contributions that will be made by the applicant or third parties to support project expenses that appear in the budget. Include in this amount third-party cash gifts that will be raised to release Federal matching funds. (Consult the program guidelines for information on cost-sharing requirements.)

[3]Indicate the amount of actual or anticipated awards from other Federal agencies for this project and this grant period only.

[4]Total Project Funding should equal Total Project Costs.

Institutional Grant Administrator

Indicate the name, title, address, and phone number of the person who will be responsible for the actual financial administration of the grant if the award is made—e.g., ensuring compliance with the terms and conditions of the award, submitting financial status reports.

S. C. Row, Assistant Comptroller
_____   Telephone (100) 222-4444
Name and Title (Please type or print)   _____
                                                                       area code

100 Yellow Brick Road, Emerald City, OZ 00000
_____   Date   9/25/89
Address   _____

Form courtesy the National Historical Publications and Records Commission.

integral part of the repository, participating in normal staff activities and receiving standard benefits. Careful selection, supervision, and nurturing will allow grant staff to complete their assigned tasks on schedule.

Funding agencies judge repositories not only on the basis of the value and creativity of the grants that are submitted, but also on the repository's ability to carry out successfully the tasks which they have proposed. Grant management plays an important role in insuring that the program is completed on time and within the budget and should not be overlooked by archival administrators.

Conclusion

As a manager, the archival administrator is responsible for ensuring that the archives has sufficient resources to achieve its goals. Financial support is critical to success, but it is frequently inadequate. Through planning, financial analysis, and persuasion, archival administrators can increase funding and expand archival opportunities for their institutions by using imagination, research, and resourcefulness.

Suggested Readings

Thomas E. Broce, *Fund Raising, The Guide To Raising Money From Private Sources* (Norman, Okla.: University of Oklahoma Press, 1986) is a good introduction to fund-raising techniques. For information on private foundations, the best single source is The Foundation Center, *The Foundation Directory* (New York: The Foundation Center, 1987). This can be supplemented by The Foundation Center, *The Foundation Directory Supplement* (New York: The Foundation Center, 1989); Denise Wallen and Karen Cantrell, *Funding for Museums, Archives and Special Collections* (Phoenix, Ariz.: Oryx Press, 1988); and National Register Publishing Company, *Annual Register of Grant Support: A Directory of Funding Sources* (Washington, D.C.: National Register Publishing Company, 1987).

Other sources of information covering both public and private funds include: David J. Hauman, *The Capital Campaign Handbook: How to Maximize Your Fund Raising Campaign* (Washington, D.C.: The Taft Group, 1987); Virginia White, *Grant Proposals That Succeeded* (Washington, D.C.: American Association of Museums, 1983); and Paul Schneiter and Donald Nelson, *The Thirteen Most Common Fund Raising Mistakes and How To Avoid Them* (Washington, D.C.: American Association of Museums, 1982).

A useful article in the archival literature is Timothy Walch, "The Archivist's Search For Grant Funding," *Provenance* 1 (Spring 1983), pp. 71–77.

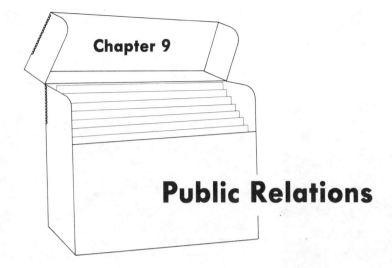

Chapter 9

Public Relations

Public relations refers to the communication or dialogue which a repository has with individuals or groups inside and outside its institutional setting intended to convey information about services and goals. Communication can take a variety of forms: press releases, conversations between researchers and reference archivists, or annual reports prepared for the repository's parent institution, for example. Communication must be part of a well-planned program designed to explain the archives' mission and involve people in its program. Public relations is an integral part of management. It must be a deliberate effort and should be included in the long-range planning process. Public relations must begin with a clear understanding of the repository's mission and its various publics.

In developing a public relations program, an archival administrator must distinguish between public relations, public programs, and outreach. Public relations is concerned with communication between the repository and its public in whatever form that communication may take. Public programs and outreach are educational and marketing tools that provide products and services to varied audiences. However, such efforts should fall under the overall rubric of public relations so that such efforts lead toward a better understanding of the archives and its mission.

Archival Image

One of the purposes of archival public relations programs is the establishment of an appropriate image. Archivists must convince their public and their employers that their work is of significant value to the parent institution. According to studies done by the Society of American Archivists, archivists are often seen as helpful, but not vital, to the overall institutional mission. Is it any wonder then, that when an institutional budget crunch comes, or new management is looking for ways to improve profits, that archives is often one of the first departments to be cut?

The image that archivists want to project to employers, researchers, and to the public will depend to some degree upon whether the program is an institutional archives or a manuscripts repository. Whatever the situation, archivists should strive to make clear that they provide a fast and dynamic service, that they have sources which no one else can provide, and that they are a department which the institution cannot do without. This is a tall order, but archivists who provide these services and use appropriate public relations techniques can work to achieve this goal.

Developing Constituencies

Successful archival programs develop large and loyal constituencies, groups of people with vested interests in the repository. They may be people who supervise the archives program, approve its budget, sit on its advisory board, use its holdings, read its newsletter, donate material to its collection, or think that having an archives is a worthwhile idea. Their support may develop for emotional or practical reasons.

Archivists must begin by developing a plan for reaching those within their own organization,

The image archivists project is vital to the future health and well-being of the archives. *(Toby Talbot, courtesy Vermont State Archives)*

An archivist using historical records while speaking to a group of school children contributes to a valuable public relations effort. *(New York State Archives and Records Administration)*

whether the repository is part of a business, university, state government, or not-for-profit agency. An internal public relations program can take on many different faces, but whatever is envisaged, it should achieve the goal of making the archives an integral part of its parent organization.

Efforts may include assisting the public relations department by providing information, photographs, or other materials, writing articles for in-house and public consumption, providing information to the personnel department for new staff orientation, developing exhibits, or other projects which publicize the value and importance of the archives. If well done, these internal efforts cultivate a large and growing group of archival supporters who better understand the mission of the archives. Whatever the level of interest or involvement, it is important that administrators and staff of the parent institution have a positive image of the program. They will feel this way only if the exhibits they see

are professional and engaging, if the reference service they receive is thorough, if collections are processed thoroughly and efficiently, or if they hear about the repository in a positive way from someone who has had contact with it. In these examples the archives is cultivating individuals who are more likely to support its future endeavors. Success may not assure that the repository will achieve all its goals or get more funding, but failure to communicate is likely to lead to an unappreciated and underfunded program.

In addition to developing internal support from their parent institutions, many repositories must develop constituencies outside the parent institutions. Public interest and support for the archival program is valuable for a number of reasons. First and foremost, good public relations will assist the repository in developing financial support. If an archives is a vital community resource or valued by members of the public as a respected cultural center, this image should assist it in developing financial support from its parent organization or the public agency with funding responsibility. Second, a good public image will assist the repository in developing its collections and acquiring useful material. Third, public interest should increase use of the archives' collections.

The emphasis on internal versus external constituencies will vary depending upon the type of archival institution. An institutional or business archives will focus its primary efforts on developing internal constituencies since most of its funding comes from its parent institution. A manuscripts repository, on the other hand, must develop external constituencies which see the value of its mission and provide moral and financial support. A state ar-

Painter Jacob Lawrence (left), recipient of the Second Annual Amistad Fine Arts Award, talks to Clifton H. Johnson (right), executive director of the Amistad Research Center. The Fine Arts Award involves leaders of the fine arts community in New Orleans, and the award ceremony itself draws sizeable contributions from benefactors, sponsors, and patrons. (Lester Sullivan, courtesy Amistad Research Center, Tulane University)

chives must balance an internal constituency of government employees with the tax-paying public.

One of the goals of the archival manager should be to tailor the public relations program to the interests of various constituencies, strengthening the bonds of support between them and the archival program. This will not be an easy task since each group looks on the repository from a totally different perspective. Nonetheless, it is a task worth pursuing. If successful, the manager will know where to turn when the archives needs financial, institutional, or other support. The ability to draw on people with a vested interest in the program is a strong advantage.

Planning a Public Relations Program

In developing a public relations program, the archival administrator should use the planning guidelines outlined in Chapter 4. Plans should evolve from the mission statement that defines not only program goals but the constituencies for which the archives is responsible.

Planning should begin with market research to discover the constituencies which the repository should reach. After constituencies are identified, administrators need further research to identify consumer needs and develop a range of programs to meet them. Once this preliminary work is complete, the archivist should develop goals, objectives, and activities for an overall public relations program which includes an evaluation component to ensure

that the programs are meeting institutional and public needs.

Public Relations Staff

The manager must first decide who will have overall responsibility for public relations. Public relations work requires skills in writing and interpersonal relations, and the person responsible should be carefully selected with these factors in mind. Only the very largest repositories will be able to assign someone to carry out public relations responsibilities on a full-time basis. In most institutions, public relations naturally fall within the archival administrator's responsibility. However, given the importance of this function, other alternatives should be considered. Staff members with skills or experience in this area could be given this task as one of their responsibilities. Another possibility is the appointment of an experienced volunteer as the public relations representative.

Whoever is responsible should work closely with the parent institution's public relations department or officer. The repository must coordinate its public relations effort with the parent institution, building on the success of programs which are already started while not interfering with media or other relationships which have already been established. At the same time the archives should take advantage of the public relations department's expertise and its contacts outside the parent institution setting.

Developing a Good Public Relations Attitude

To develop a good program, a repository must take public relations seriously. Public relations cannot, however, operate in a vacuum. A public relations program is only as good as the program it is publicizing. In business, excellent advertising has a difficult time selling a poorly designed or poorly manufactured product, and a poor archival program will meet the same fate. Standards must also be set for the material produced by the institution. Guidelines for writing and design should be established to govern the development of new publications prepared for public relations use.

Archival public relations programs should begin by ensuring that the services they offer are of high quality. Staff must know that the work they do is important and has an impact on those who come into contact with the archives. A pleasant, well-designed research room, knowledgeable staff with a welcoming demeanor, and easily accessible and usable finding aids send a positive signal to persons using the resources. In whatever setting, whether assisting researchers, leading tours, or giving speeches, staff must be encouraged to behave in a friendly, courteous, and professional manner. All staff must understand how each individual can personally aid a public relations effort.

Marketing Archival Services

Public relations reach a public which has little initial interest or information about archives. Few people have any experience using archives and must be educated to the value of both the collections and services. In addition, archivists must overcome a built-in reticence on the part of their users. Because few people use archives and have only a vague image of their value or content, their fear of the unknown must be overcome. Marketing techniques used by repositories must emphasize their user-friendliness. This means not only that they are easily accessible, but also that there is information in archives which people need and can readily use. Archivists must look at their procedures and collections from a user's viewpoint if they are to sell their product effectively.

If institutional archives are to market their programs successfully, they must carefully examine their institutional environment. Who are the resource allocators that must be moved to support the archives, and what is the most effective manner to reach them? Who uses archival services? Who could use archival services, but does not? What are the characteristics of their institutional culture? How are they best reached? The archives must communicate with all of these audiences if it is to gain their support. Archival administrators must understand their own institutional culture, its vocabulary, and methodology and plan the outreach program to fit a specific setting. Such reviews should include all programs: publications, donor relations, exhibitions, or records management.

Manuscript repositories must approach this situation in a similar fashion. However, their task is more complicated since their resource allocators and intended audience are likely to be less specific and more diverse. Public relations efforts may require using one vocabulary and methodology with one audience and one quite different for another. While this may make manuscript administrators' tasks more difficult, it should not deter them from designing specific public relations programs for particular audiences.

The William Warfield exhibit was arranged for a ceremony celebrating the presentation of his papers to Amistad Research Center. *(Andrew Simms, courtesy Amistad Research Center, Tulane University)*

Market research can be carried out in a number of ways. One method is through oral or written surveys. Surveys can be designed to study the needs of researchers or persons using other services such as records management. To be effective, questions must be open-ended and provide the person an opportunity to criticize or offer useful suggestions: How could service be improved? Was the system of finding aids easily understandable? Were records manuals useful? Was the information that was needed readily accessible?

If the repository is producing a brochure to publicize its services, it should decide to whom it will be directed. To ensure that the brochure is effective, the archival administrator could select a representative group of people to review the brochure during the writing and design phases. Participants in the test market can respond from their specific perspectives ensuring that the brochure communicates with the audience it is designed to serve. All archival public relations programs should have a market research component and require continuing feedback so that they meet audience needs.

Targeting Audiences

When developing a public relations message, the archives must carefully decide which audience it wishes to reach and the method which will most effectively communicate with that particular group. For example, a brochure designed for fund raising will probably look quite different from one designed to introduce researchers to a repository's collection and services. Similarly, articles written for the parent institution's publications can assume certain levels of knowledge that would be unwise in a public press release.

Archival administrators must develop a well-designed plan to reach a particular group. Such a plan must take into account the audience, the message, and the medium used to convey the message.

Since archives are usually short of both staff and money there is a great temptation to develop public relations efforts that send one message to all audiences. Although this approach may be better than sending no message at all, the public relations program will be more effective if it can send specific communications to specific audiences.

Press Releases

To extend its message beyond those people who visit, the repository must make its presence known to the wider community. Effective use of newspapers, radio, and television is an important means of reaching beyond the repository. Press releases are a proven means of distributing information to the media. Press releases can announce major donations, the opening of a new collection, lectures or exhibitions open to the public, instructional classes, or provide general information or historical background about current events.

Press releases generally follow a standard format. They should be typed and double spaced and answer the questions of who, what, where, when, and why. (See Figure 9-1.) The press release should be clear and concise. It should be positive and encourage people to participate in whatever type of program is being publicized. If funds are available, the archives should send one or more accompanying photographs illustrating the release, since this may encourage the newspaper to print the article. The name, address, and telephone number of the repository should be included along with the name of the person who can provide additional information about the event.

Good Media Relations

Press releases may provide information to the media, but they will not ensure that the message is distributed. Newspapers, radio, and television are inundated by press releases and must select those which they feel are of the greatest interest to their audience. If the message is to reach the public, archival administrators or the responsible staff must develop a close working relationship with the media. They should discover who covers historical or cultural organizations and attempt to become better

Figure 9-1

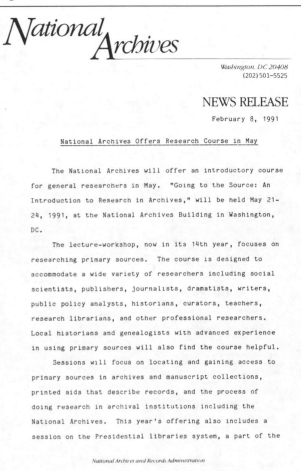

Courtesy of National Archives and Records Administration.

acquainted with them. Providing reporters with general information about the archival program and inviting them to visit the repository will help them to understand the archives' mission and to place future press releases into an appropriate context. The repository can offer to provide additional background information about particular stories or current events. By cultivating reporters, the archives increases the likelihood that its stories receive adequate coverage and makes it more probable that the reporters themselves will initiate requests to do feature stories or articles.

Other Media

Newspapers are one form of communicating information about the archival program, but archivists must look beyond this medium. Both radio and television offer useful avenues of communication. Talk radio stations in many areas increasingly seek infor-

★ ★ ★ MIDWEST EDITION MONDAY, JANUARY 16, 1989 SHARON, PENNSYLVANIA

Companies Plumb the Past to Protect the Present

When Mount St. Helens erupted in Washington in 1980, Weyerhaeuser was faced with the enormous task of salvaging downed timber. The extent of the damage reminded old-timers at Weyerhaeuser of Typhoon Frieda in 1962, when even more timber was downed.

Fortunately, the company had established archives in 1974, and documents relating to the earlier disaster's salvage operations were readily available. Weyerhaeuser based its Mount St. Helens operations on this information, and employed 650 loggers and 600 trucks over three years to complete the job.

Also in 1980, Texas Pacific Land Trust Certificate Number 390 surfaced in Wells Fargo's five-year-old archives in San Francisco. The most famous missing trust certificate in U.S. history was spotted by an alert archivist in a box of documents recovered from a Manhattan subbasement.

Worth only a few hundred dollars when lost at the turn of the century, the certificate was worth $5 million when found. Wells Fargo's archivists also helped document transactions relating to it. Three medical schools and an elderly woman were the successful claimants to the money, and the company got good publicity for its frontier slogan, "Wells Fargo never forgets!"

Businesses hire professional archivists to select essential records and discard unnecessary ones—an alternative to destroying too much too soon, saving too much too long, or just automatically saving records to certain dates and then destroying them. Borden Inc., a century-old multinational corporation, hired an archival consultant last year to begin assembling an archives. So far, he has located 150 cubic feet of historic material, most found in the public-relations department.

Are the benefits of archives felt only in once-in-a-lifetime discoveries? Not at all. Take the executive-search area. A major financial-services firm, looking for a new CEO, spent several months and thousands of dollars collecting and analyzing information on past successful executive searches. This information could have been at management's fingertips in well-run archives. Business archives also provide easier access to critical information

Manager's Journal

By Ellen NicKenzie Lawson

needed by management in litigation, sales, acquisitions, and for sound managerial judgment.

Having archives can be useful when your company is in sales and acquisitions negotiations, too. The archives can be a specified asset, or the buyer can retain the archives or donate it to a non-profit museum or university as a tax write-off. When the Cleveland Press was purchased a few years ago, the buyer reportedly took a substantial write-off by donating the entire news clipping and photographic collection—covering 80 years of city history—to the Cleveland State University library.

Purchasers are in a better position to absorb records of the acquired company if they have archives of their own. Procter & Gamble has acquired four major businesses in the 1980s: Orange Crush, Norwich Eaton Pharmaceuticals, Folger Coffee, and Richardson-Vicks Inc. Corporation archivist Ed Rider has seen that the records of each acquired company are properly accounted for in the wake of each takeover. Mr. Rider was hired in 1980 after Procter & Gamble's management realized the need for an up-to-date archives when encountering problems locating data—particularly for the past 25 years—to celebrate the company's 150th anniversary. Mr. Rider warns others to "keep archives current for future use instead of operating on

an 'anniversary mentality.' "

Since 1981, Procter & Gamble has created and distributed, at cost, more than 100,000 copies of teaching units for high-school social studies courses. The unit on World War II includes memos, letters and newsletters from the archives that bring to life important social changes and developments. These include the feminization of the company's work force in wartime; the seriousness of employee bond drives; the discontinuance of certain products during the war; and how American business cooperated with the government in running ordnance plants for national defense. Assuming each teacher uses a unit in one classroom with 30 students, the company has been able to reach more than three million potential consumers of its products.

Of course, the costs of an archives must also be considered: salary for a trained archivist; storage space that is fireproof, waterproof and secure; and office support. In the short run, costs can be covered by transferring funds from the budgets of those most benefiting from an archives: the legal, public relations, and records departments.

Outsiders can be charged user fees, and their access should be limited to non-confidential records. Sporting News, based in St. Louis, charges user fees for reproductions of photographs from its historical sports collection. While its archives have yet to make a profit, costs were covered last year by these user fees. Other businesses provide services to outsiders gratis as corporate good will.

In the long run, well-planned, well-run corporate archives may pay for themselves. The University of Akron acquired the papers of Firestone in 1986 just prior to Firestone's sale to the Japanese and change of headquarters to Chicago. The benefits to Akron of retaining the history of this corporation, which helped make the city the rubber capital of the world, are in-

calculable in terms of local history.

When a corporation donates archives to a non-profit institution, the corporation might also consider targeting corporate gifts toward that institution to cover the archives' maintenance costs. Such a gift would do double-duty as a means of preserving the firm's own history.

Of course, business managers know that any cost-benefit analysis of archives assumes an understanding that history, for its own sake, has a value—although this is hard to calculate in dollars and cents. In an era of information overload and rapid change, a sense of history gives stability and continuity. Businesses with no sense of the past project weak corporate images into the future.

Ms. Lawson, a historical consultant in Cleveland Heights, Ohio, is organizing archives at Cleveland's National City Bank.

An archivist's effort to encourage a general interest in archives. *(Ellen N. Lawson)*

mation on a variety of topics and can increase public knowledge through the use of the talk-back format. The advent of cable television offers yet another avenue to publicize events and archival collections, and in many cases, time is available for the asking. Cable channels are sometimes on the air at odd hours or for a limited time, but they do offer the repository an opportunity to communicate with a large, untapped audience.

Finally, archivists should take advantage of the lower cost and increasing availability of video presentations. With audiences accustomed to receiving information primarily through television, archivists must develop means of communicating with them. Videotapes can be prepared for use on television, with small groups, or for use by individuals in their own homes. With careful planning, videotapes can become another useful public relations tool.

Archival Publications

In order to meet the specific needs of its different clienteles, the repository must develop publica-

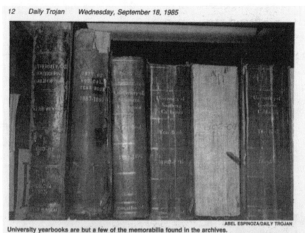

University yearbooks are but a few of the memorabilia found in the archives.

ABEL ESPINOZA/DAILY TROJAN

Treasure trove of university history lies buried in Doheny

By Bob Ickes
Staff Writer

Buried within the bowels of Doheny Library lies a treasure trove of Trojan history — 1,500 square feet of scrapbooks, yearbooks and priceless memorabilia stored in a cage called the University Archives.

Though its resources are bountiful, its location is remote. Housed on the Doheny stacks' bottom level, and accessible only by special elevator key, the archives is far removed from the hectic activity of the floors above it.

"Things move slower down here," said Paul Christopher, university archivist.

"We're not concerned with day-to-day requests for curriculum-related information. We are, in a sense, the memory of the university. We preserve its past so decision-makers can learn from it and plan the future," he said.

Archives patrons are a diverse group, including publishers, alumni, scholars and history buffs. They come from across the country and around the world. Many place requests

through the mail and over the phone.

Christopher assists them in research projects that range from helping adopted children search old enrollment lists for their natural parents to providing the dates of more than 100 landmark events for a USC trivia calendar.

Class reunions are enhanced by the nostalgic slide shows Christopher offers; he jogs alumni memories with his selections from the 8,000 archives photos and negatives. His latest

(Continued on page 22)

Archives stores memories

(Continued from page 12)

project — the class of 1960's 25th reunion in October.

Among Christopher's proudest archival possessions is the complete set of personal papers he has for all USC presidents since 1947.

Also available are every edition of the *El Rodeo* since 1899, the first year of publication; every issue of the *Daily Trojan* since the first one in 1912 (as well as its predecessors, which date to the 1880s) and Christopher's own "ephemera file," an exhaustive collection of clippings, photos and mementos that shed light upon all aspects of university life.

The archives has been a traveling history show, moving three times since 1977. It began in a vault beneath a Doheny staircase and moved to a basement room before settling in its present location in 1984.

As the university continues to

grow, so will the archives, and Christopher sees another move in his future. But where he'll be going is anybody's guess.

Christopher has been the full-time archivist since 1983. Before that, his position, and archives interest on campus, was decidedly part-time. He calls his job a "joy," one that demands attention to detail and a love of history.

"I'm always impressed by the enthusiasm and respect that archives patrons demonstrate toward our material. I am delighted to assist them," he said.

Christopher would also be delighted if the school would designate the archives the official repository of all university-related documents.

"That way, things would be centralized — there wouldn't be hundreds of miniature archives in offices all across the campus," he said. His wish list doesn't

stop there.

"University officials need to realize the historical importance of the materials with which they work. So many times the archives has lost to the trash important potential resources because people have thought, 'I didn't think you'd be interested in that.' "

Hanging on a partition are original nails used in the construction of the oldest building on campus, what is now the Widney Alumni House.

Next to those is a protest leaflet distributed during the early '70s, urging students to boycott classes and let their voices be heard.

Nearby is a chart that details the university's dramatic rise in enrollment over the years, from the handful of students here in the 1880s to the thousands that attend in 1985.

Articles about university archives can create interest on campus and increase use of the facility. *(Paul Christopher, courtesy University of Southern California Archives)*

tions to communicate its services and activities. Published brochures can be especially designed to market particular programs. One all-purpose brochure may meet the needs of small institutions, while large institutions should develop specialized brochures which inform researchers about archival services, encourage and inform potential donors of archival material, publicize archival publications, or

inform users of specialized services such as records management.

In drafting an all-purpose brochure designed for a number of uses, the archives must carefully consider its audiences and include information which meets all of their needs. By considering the differing needs of donors and researchers, the repository can create a relatively low-cost, effective tool which promotes its services. A brochure usually includes the repository's mission statement, address, telephone number, hours, and a map. It should be simply worded avoiding technical language. It should be attractively designed and contain as many photographs and illustrations as the archives can afford. The brochure can be easily distributed by enclosing it in reference replies and letters requesting donations, including it as a newsletter insert, giving it to institutional employees with their payroll checks, sending it by special mailings to other cultural or historical organizations in the same geographical area, and placing it in brochure racks at the Chamber of Commerce, the public library, or other public places.

Newsletters

A newsletter can meet a number of informational needs. It can inform people of archival activities, provide dates for upcoming events, give news about new collections or collection openings, and provide historical or biographical articles. Its content must be designed for the intended audience: employees of the archives' parent institution or a more general audience including donors, users, and interested members of the public. (See Figure 9-2).

A newsletter cannot be produced without some expense, but costs can be kept to a minimum. A photocopy machine combined with either a typewriter or inexpensive desktop publisher can produce an attractive newsletter at minimal cost. If the newsletter is an internal publication, its distribution cost will be negligible. Postage costs for external publications can be lowered by using a postal permit for bulk mail.

Published Reports

A written annual report is yet another method of "communicating the archives' story," although it is often overlooked as a public relations tool by archival managers. An annual report can be aimed at a number of different audiences depending upon the repository's institutional affiliation. It can be strictly an internal document to show a parent organization

Figure 9-2

Newsletters representing a variety of institutions (left to right): a manuscript repository *(American Heritage Center)*; a state archives *(New York State Archives and Records Administration)*; and an institutional archives *(The Salvation Army Archives and Research Center).*

the archives' current status, achievements, and future needs. An annual report, however, can be an important tool for communicating the role and importance of the repository to administrators who have the archives as part of their responsibility. It should be attractive, brief, and distributed as widely as possible within the institutional hierarchy and to peers in other departments.

The annual report should be closely related to the repository's long-range plan and provide a means of measuring progress and revising the plan in view of institutional successes or failures. It should include statistical measurements of activities in which the archives is engaged. But it can also include anecdotal information, showing the impact of research in archives. By providing such information on a long-term basis, the archives can document such trends as reference use or acquisition and communicate needs to a variety of constituencies.

Publishing a brief, illustrated annual report intended for a wider audience is another useful public relations tool. A report designed for nonspecialists should be general and nontechnical in content. It should highlight the value of the repository through photographs, illustrations, and graphs which make archival functions understandable to the lay person.

A successful report should encourage archival use while at the same time creating archival pride.

Conclusion

The list of possible public relations programs and activities is nearly endless and is only restrained by the imagination and budget of the archivist. Clearly, not every activity mentioned in this chapter will be done by every repository. Archival managers, however, should plan an ongoing public relations program to help meet the archives' overall goals.

Public relations are critical in developing support for the archival program. With the information overload felt by individuals in modern society, people will not go out of their way to learn about new programs or new ideas. Because archives are not thoroughly understood, archivists bear an additional burden which requires an even greater effort than that of fellow professionals found in cultural agencies such as libraries and museums. Information about archives must be brought to people in a familiar and understandable way. Failure to build support for the archives through a public relations program may lead not only to a lack of funding, but also to the demise of the program itself. Successful archival managers must find ways for their programs not only to survive, but also to prosper, and this can only be done through a planned and thorough public relations program.

Suggested Readings

Although somewhat dated, the following are the most complete and thorough volumes available on archival outreach: Ann E. Pederson and Gail Farr Casterline, *Archives and Manuscripts: Public Programs* (Chicago: Society of American Archivists, 1982), and Gail Farr Casterline, *Archives and Manuscripts: Exhibits* (Chicago: Society of American Archivists, 1980).

Other archival publications include Ann E. Pederson, ed., *Keeping Archives* (Sydney, Australia: Australian Society of Archivists, 1987), pp. 313–354. Maygene Daniels and Timothy Walch, eds., *A Modern Archives Reader* (Washington, D.C.: National Archives and Records Service, 1984) puts public programs into a management context. (See Chapter 8.)

Books from related professions include International Council of Museums, *Public View: The ICOM Handbook of Museum Public Relations* (Paris: International Council of Museums, 1986); and G. Donald Adams, *Museum Public Relations* (Nashville: American Association for State and Local History, 1983).

Chapter 10

Technology and the Archival Manager

Technology will present archival managers with the most volatile component of their external environment. Computers control various aspects of archival operations; in addition, machine-readable records are confronting archival managers with opportunities and challenges at least as demanding as any externally imposed condition of the last fifty to seventy-five years. Related technologies in telecommunications, including the use of electronic mail and facsimile machines, are changing the ways organizations communicate, with significant effect on patterns of records creation and retention.

How does the manager evaluate a new technology—or the application of a familiar technology not currently in an institution? How does a manager determine that a technique or equipment is worth an investment of time, personnel, money, or even floor space, all of which, in the typical archival situation, are likely to be severely limited? These can be difficult questions even in technologically static conditions; they are more complicated in an uncertain environment.

This chapter will not provide archival managers with an introduction to computers or any other technology. Other sources are available to do that with far more expertise than would be possible here. Moreover, managing technology is not the same as becoming expert in that technology. This is not to propose that technical ignorance is bliss, but merely to suggest that managers and technical experts have different perspectives from which they need to judge technologies.

For the manager, technology is a tool or set of tools, acquired and used to achieve a stated objective.

The tools may be as simple as shelving or as sophisticated as automated information systems. It may be an advantage to know something about the various (and possibly competing) technologies available to achieve the objective, but managers should not become so enamored of the tools that they lose sight of the objective. For example, shelving multiplies available floor space and helps preserve records, both desirable objectives in an archival setting. The archival manager should know enough about shelving to deal with the ways in which various types or sizes of shelving help accomplish these goals, and he or she may even want to know about some of the relative advantages and disadvantages (or "trade-offs") of each. The manager does not need a technician's understanding of how to install or maintain shelving.

The technology of greatest concern to archivists is the computer and the various information media driven by advances in computer design and applications. Though much of what follows could be said about managing any technology, the focus will be on the computer.

Information System Management

An archives is an information system: a set of arrangements, tools, and personnel assembled to acquire, store, manage, and retrieve information. Consistent with systems theory, an information system should benefit from the integration of its various parts into a sensible whole and provide collectively more value than the sum value of its individual components. Any information system—manual or automated—includes procedures and equipment for identifying, acquiring, processing, storing, and retrieving information. Recognition of this virtual truism should simplify the archival manager's adjustment to a new technology and provide some confidence that—once the specific procedures and techniques associated with the new technology are identified and absorbed—an archival institution should be able to adapt to its new technical environment successfully. One useful skill for the archival manager who hopes to make technological change more of an opportunity than a threat is an understanding of the process by which systems are planned and acquired.

Systems Planning and Acquisition

Systems planning involves a sequence of phases. For purposes of this manual, a relatively simplified process, outlined below, will be used.

- Requirements
  - —functional requirements
  - —current capabilities
  - —cost and scheduling requirements
- System design
  - —implementation
  - —evaluation

Whether an archival manager's situation and budget dictate the need for a single personal computer, a networked mainframe, or something in between, the same sequence can and should apply.

Requirements

Why does an organization want a new information system? What is the system supposed to do? Who will use the new system, and what are their needs? Will the users of the system have the skills to operate it? The answers to these questions represent the system's requirements.

System planning involves the interaction of persons or organizations who will use the system and designers who will translate requirements specified by the users into an operational system. In many archival settings, the two roles may well be played by the same person. The one-person staff may be responsible for determining that a new systems capability is required, defining what that system should be, training himself or herself in its use, and ultimately using the system. Expert assistance may take the form of nothing more than the advice of salespersons at the local computer store.

Before plunging into design and development, the manager needs to remember that gaining access to a new capability may not always entail buying or developing a new system. Sharing an existing system is an important option, especially where communication from one organization or institution to another is important. The same is true even for something as simple as choosing word processing software. If a university archives, for example, sends frequent reports, memoranda, and other correspondence to other parts of the university, it should strongly consider acquiring the software package in use by the other units with which it deals.

At the risk of stating the obvious, it must be noted that requirements should be identified before a system is designed or acquired. Obvious or not, this bit of wisdom is often ignored. It may be tempting to assume, based on testimony from a satisfied colleague, that the virtues of a system are so self-evident as to eliminate the need for the articulation of requirements. Avoid this temptation. The successful use of a system in one organization is no assurance that the system would prove successful in a similar organization.

It is possible to be too precise in defining requirements, inhibiting the designers from considering a full range of possible solutions. A requirement that specifies "the archives needs an optical disk system" may be valid, but identifying requirements in functional terms ("the archives needs a more compact storage method for infrequently used records") is a better way to ensure the evaluation of all available options, some of which are likely to be cheaper and more efficient than others. More often, however, system failures result from lack of precision. "What do you want the system to do?" "Automate our operations." "How do you want it to work?" "Fast." This dialogue is not a likely prescription for success.

Functional Requirements. The user needs to take the lead in defining *functional* requirements; the system designer should have primary responsibility for identifying the system that will meet those requirements. Archival managers and their staffs, especially those with limited technical backgrounds, should resist the tendency to respond to the question of what kind of system they want with an answer like "An IBM PC-based local area net with eight outstations, each of which should have five megabyte local hard disk storage and access to a central storage or file server with four hundred megabyte capacity." A more appropriate answer should emphasize the type of work that is being automated, the volume of data involved, the number of persons or workstations that need to be connected, and so on.

If the archivist is fortunate enough to obtain the services of a system designer from outside the archives staff, it is important to determine the designer's experience with—and understanding of—archival procedures and techniques. Referrals from colleagues and from other parts of a parent institution may be helpful. It may also help to let the designer see how the function being modernized is currently performed.

The process of defining requirements must include a statement of their priority. Which is more important in a computer system: storage capacity or retrieval speed? How much of a premium is the organization prepared to spend to increase one capability over another? Costs need to be measured not just in dollar terms, but in the probable loss of capability in one area to emphasize another. Timeliness is not likely to have as high a priority for archivists as it may have for some other computer applications. Ease of use ("friendliness") may be more important. This can be especially true if the prospective users of the system have little experience with computers, if the organization has limited training resources available, or if the system is to be made available for researchers.

The manager dealing with systems design must make certain that all parts of the user population are included in requirements definition. One may not wish to stimulate conflicts between researchers and staff members, or professional staff versus clerical staff, but if differences in need or emphasis are going to occur, it is preferable to identify them early in the planning process, while it is still possible to eliminate or minimize them. A survey of the constituencies that claim a voice in a system's design can reduce later problems and can also assist in the development of advocates who may be useful in acquiring resources for the project.

An important part of a requirements definition is a statement of how the requirements are currently being met, meaning both in what way and how effectively they are being performed. Though a review of current procedures is often described as a separate stage in project development, or in overall institutional planning, it can fit nicely in a requirements phase. An understanding of the techniques and procedures used to perform a function in one technology can be useful in designing a follow-on system. Even though the purpose of system design is to provide a tool that achieves stated objectives, and not to copy established procedures, this can be an area of some flexibility. Retaining some aspects of standard procedure and work flow not only assists in providing operational continuity, but also reduces the time and effort required to acquaint users with the new system. It can also reduce the resistance the new system encounters from users accustomed to an established way of doing things.

What if the review of current operations reveals major operational or procedural shortcomings, beyond those technical limitations likely to be solved with a new system? Managers must be realistic about what any technology can do—and cannot do. No computer (and no other tool, for that matter) is likely to solve fundamental problems in staffing (whether in the size of a staff or its capabilities), purpose, organizational structure, or other basic management functions. In fact, the introduction of a new, and possibly controversial, technology can generate significant stress and uncertainty in employees, making existing problems worse. "When in doubt, automate!" is a poor motto for the archival manager. The manager whose requirements study reveals major problems or uncertainties in performing the fundamental tasks of an organization should consider postponing major systems enhancements until the organization's house is in at least reasonable order.

Cost and Scheduling Requirements

In addition to functional requirements, project planning needs to consider cost and scheduling. Getting higher authority to agree that additional equipment would be "nice to have" is meaningless if they have no intention of providing money to buy it. Scheduling is also important, and must be linked to the institution's overall plans. If an archives is planning to move into another facility, at what point should it stop improving its current space? In establishing both cost and scheduling requirements, the archival manager must have a sense of the limits reality will impose on any project. These limits should not be seen as fixed or permanent, and the successful archival manager may, over time, redefine those limits in the archives' favor. Such expectations should not, however, interfere with the manager's sense of what is possible in the short term.

System Design

At this stage, the archival manager turns over more of the responsibility for the project to the system designer. At every point, nonetheless, the design needs to correspond with the objectives stated by the repository and the cost and schedule guidelines established for the project. A system that performs spectacular technical feats in the eyes of its designer but does not meet the requirements set for it by its user does not, by definition, work well.

The first goal of any design effort is determining whether the requirements can be met within the limitations established for the project. This is a feasibility assessment. What problems are to be solved? What benefits are to result from the project? Is technology available to meet the established requirements? Can the system be developed within the time and resource limits established by or imposed on the customer?

Whether the design effort is being undertaken by the repository's own staff or through outside experts or contractors, design must be an interactive process. The manager will need to have a contract, formal or otherwise, in which the designers agree to provide the manager with reports of their progress.[1] A feasibility assessment is one such report.

Once the feasibility analysis is in hand, the manager will need to make decisions. Every system involves compromises between cost, capability, and scheduling. The feasibility study may indicate that the requirements can be met within the current technical state of the art, but that the cost would be 30 percent more than the repository planned to spend. The manager *may* then have a choice: Can the price be brought into line by reducing or eliminating requirements? Maybe, given that systems usually can be modified to provide a solution to a problem, even if it is not an ideal solution. If the choice is to reduce requirements, however, the manager must ask whether accepting a system with reduced capabilities is worth the cost and the effort. The other alternative, of course, is to come up with additional money to buy the full capability. This can be far more easily said than done. In reality, the only choice the manager may have is to accept a reduced system or continue with the status quo.

Trade-offs in scheduling involve similar decision making. "Do you want it right, or do you want it tomorrow?" is the way some engineers put this dilemma. Designers and programmers, whether in-house or contractors, can be busy people, and archival projects are often smaller, less profitable, or less prestigious than other projects available to them. To what degree can scheduling be modified to reflect this?

One problem archival managers will face is that newer technologies will be developed during project design. When should the manager consider dropping one design and moving on to newer technology? Only in the rare instance when time and money lost in such reversals are outweighed by the benefits of the newer technology. There is no point in delaying a project until the arrival of the perfect technology. Some degree of obsolescence will be built into any system, thus putting a premium on systems with the flexibility to accept later enhancements or adaptations. Archival managers, who will want information in their care to be available for periods far exceeding those of other users, have a critical interest in such flexibility and in the development of standards and protocols to permit the migration of information across several generations of technology.

The feasibility study brings the manager to a major decision point. Assuming that the study has determined that the project can be accomplished, its review should result in modification of either the system or the requirements and in a decision to proceed or not to proceed. Before this decision, the expenditure of time, effort, and money has been relatively limited. Once management accepts the feasibility study, this will change.

Once feasibility is determined and the organization has decided to proceed, the archives will prepare a request for proposal (RFP), providing detailed specifications for the project. Without an RFP, a potential supplier or vendor will not be bound by a firm statement of the customer's needs and the archives will be denied an opportunity to evaluate bids rationally and on common grounds. The design process must put everyone involved in a position to evaluate "apples against apples" (or perhaps "Apples against Apples"). Once the RFP is prepared and responses submitted by potential vendors, the archives must select a winner. If the archives is a component of a larger institution, the archival manager must know the parent organization's rules for making such decisions. In some organizations, conflict of interest laws and other regulations will remove the decision from the user. The user establishes the requirement, drafts or assists in the development of an RFP, and may evaluate proposals, but the final decision is made by a procurement office or contracts office.

Once the project is under contract, what is the role of the archival manager? First, the manager must ensure that the project schedule is met, or find out why it is not. The designers should be given project milestones, specified in the contract and marked by reports back to the manager. Second, the

---

[1] If the designer is an outside contractor, the relationship clearly needs to be formal. Where systems design is done by an in-house staff or the technical staff of a parent institution, a "contract" setting forth schedules and reporting requirements is very useful, though not legally enforceable.

manager must make certain that the specifications set forth in the proposal are followed. Finally, the manager must begin to consider the operational implications of the new system. Will its equipment (and associated personnel, if any) require additional space? What training and orientation efforts will be required for staff members or researchers?

The manager, not the system designer, is responsible for the transition from the existing way of conducting business to the new system. Given the archival "cycle of poverty," it is unlikely that additional staff will be provided to operate one system while simultaneously implementing its replacement. Putting up a "closed for systems upgrade" sign on the front door seems equally unrealistic, except for the most limited interruptions in service.

One solution is parallel operation, with existing procedures providing service while the new system is designed and installed. This creates its own problems, among them the need to provide continuing service with a system that is losing resources and support. Presumably, staff will be drawn from current operations to plan and train for the new system. Maintaining a constant level of service with declining staff, even for a short period, can be difficult.

A second managerial task will be to deal with the personnel problems that can come about during a major change in operations. Change is a difficult and risky business. The authors of one of the leading studies of organizational cultures have sardonically concluded that it "costs a fortune and takes forever."[2] Such optimism aside, a major systems change will likely bring out both the best and worst in a staff, frequently from the same people at different times. How does a manager encourage personnel to associate themselves with a new development? How does management convince staff members doing rearguard duty on the outgoing system that they will be rewarded equally with those associated with the flashy new project? Ideally, an organization would find the exact mix of pioneers and traditionalists on its staff to avoid such problems, but in the real world such miracles do not happen. The manager's job is to soften the blow of change by communicating to staff members (and to researchers, where necessary) why change is required and remind them of the benefits to be derived from it. A key element in this process is to include the personnel most affected by the transition in the process of defining change wher-

ever possible, and to exercise patience in letting people get comfortable with both the prospect and reality of change. Participation and patience can go a long way toward converting all but the most obstinate "change resisters" into people who can help make a new system work.

In short, then, the manager retains principal responsibility for ensuring that the organization—its people, its facilities, and its culture—is prepared to implement the new system.

Implementation

In this step, the new system is tested, adjusted, and, if it meets the requirements set forth in the contract or other document defining its capabilities, accepted for operational use.

Testing may take place throughout the design process at a site other than the one in which it will be used, but contracts should require that final acceptance tests be held in the system's permanent home, under conditions it is likely to encounter in the "real world." Operating a system in the designer's office or store is like testing a home appliance in the showroom. No system should be accepted until it has performed according to agreed-upon specifications in the archives.

Systems testing must be done according to predetermined standards. A storage device will hold so much data; a computer can handle a specific number of queries simultaneously; and so on. Testing also must include the "human subsystem," that is, the personnel who will actually have to operate it once it is accepted. Though allowance must be made for learning curves and adjustment during operation, a system that does not function well during a test phase needs to be looked at very carefully. If an institution is buying equipment or software from a contractor, the manager must assume that it will never receive better care than during preacceptance testing. Breakdowns should not be ignored, nor should assurances of "It will be okay once we get the bugs out!" be permitted to substitute for performance. It is one thing to extend the time available for testing; it is another to waive a requirement or specification critical to the system's performance.

One of the keys to testing and implementing any system is documentation. Even if one is dealing with a standard personal computer and off-the-shelf software, accurate documentation of acquisition, maintenance, and operations needs to be kept. If an institution is dealing with one-of-a-kind technology, especially software code, accurate, up-to-date docu-

---

[2] Terrence E. Deal and Allan A. Kennedy, *Corporate Cultures: The Rites and Rituals of Corporate Life* (Reading, Mass.: Addison-Wesley, 1982), p. 163.

mentation is essential. There can be no excuse for a manager's failure to ensure that critical documentation is maintained and that someone in the organization is responsible for its care.

Evaluation

Despite the best efforts at design and implementation, most new systems have problems. Once these are identified, the manager, in concert with the designers and the personnel operating the system, must diagnose the source of those problems and determine solutions. If the system is accepted, evaluation should continue throughout its operational life, as part of the normal process of management.

Evaluation of systems, like evaluation of personnel, must take place according to established criteria and the objectives defined by the repository for the system. The continuing process of reexamining objectives against changing environmental conditions will ultimately lead to additional or altered requirements for the system in question, at which point the whole systems planning and development process begins again.

Scheduling

Scheduling is not a phase of system development. Rather, it is a key to effective system development. Though the stages described above appear sequential, they are not completely so. It would be possible to manage a project so that one stage does not begin until the previous one is complete, but this wastes time and other resources. Project scheduling more closely resembles a relay race where planned overlap is attained at the passing of the baton by having each successive runner start up in anticipation of being caught by his or her predecessor. Project development then might look something like this:

Requirements _ _ _ _ _ _ _ _

   Design _ _ _ _ _ _ _ _ _ _ _ _ _

      Implementation/Testing _ _ _ _

        Operation/Evaluation _ _ _ _ _ _

Systems planning attempts to give order and logic to the development of new tools and techniques. Even in a small institution developing modest plans and systems, an effective development plan can ease many difficulties. Although details—or even fundamentals—of a project may change over the course of its development, careful consideration of the stages

of systems design can ensure that change produces a better system, not chaos.

Managing in a Technically Uncertain Environment

Archival managers cannot eliminate technological uncertainty from their lives; nor should they want to. The same technical factors that produce uncertainties and even threats to the established way of performing archival functions also represent opportunities for archivists to develop new ways to achieve the profession's goals: preserving the records of the past and making them available for researchers.

The challenge to the archival manager is to see change—even on a scale unprecedented in the recent history of the profession—as possibly beneficial and at least inevitable. The next step is a managerial commitment to positioning archival institutions to deal effectively with the coming changes. How does the archival manager accomplish this?

First, the manager must become more alert to the reality of change and make awareness of the external environment a high priority within the profession and its institutions. Large organizations may be able to accomplish this by devoting a small portion of their resources to research and development units. Staff and budget limitations make the establishment of such dedicated research elements impractical for most archival institutions, which must find (or develop) staff members interested in serving as antennas into the external environment, probably in addition to other responsibilities. Attendance at conferences and regular communication with colleagues facing similar challenges can be valuable ways of staying abreast of trends and developments. Those archival institutions that can afford to dedicate even limited resources to research and development efforts have an obligation to themselves—and to the smaller institutions that cannot support such efforts—to establish programs for communicating their findings to the profession.

Second, archival institutions need to become more comfortable with certain basic truths of being in an uncertain environment, the first of which is that research efforts imply, and perhaps even demand, an element of failure. Every research effort has projects that do not come to fruition. Failure is often the precursor to and a prerequisite of success. Failures also merit documentation, possibly as much as successes do. An archives that has evaluated a piece of software or a type of shelving and found either inadequate for its needs should alert its colleagues of this result.

Archival managers must be willing to dedicate staff and other resources to projects without requiring success—a hard thing to do in a profession marked by limited resources. It means that project managers must be chosen for their willingness to "champion" causes, but must not be judged, in career terms, solely on the success of those causes. Project staffs must be given the security of knowing that their organization will judge them at least as much by the quality of their effort as by its outcome.

Third, archival managers must encourage their staffs to become advocates of change rather than resisters of change. And here as elsewhere, leadership must be by example. Managers must identify those technological (and other) changes affecting their organization's future, make coping with those changes a principal organizational objective, and provide the means for the members of the organization to participate in meeting that objective. A manager who preaches the importance of computer literacy, but who does not take steps to incorporate that objective into career development and promotion systems, will quickly lose credibility, as will managers who exempt themselves from making an effort to bring their own skills and understanding into line with the projected environment.

Fourth, archival managers must become insatiable consumers of information that may assist in aligning their organizations with new technologies. Networking within the archival profession is a beginning, but archival managers need to look to the wider information profession and information industry for potential challenges and solutions to those challenges. The information environment is full of complex questions, and no one group or profession can claim to have all the answers. Archivists have experience to contribute to their colleagues in data systems, information resources management, and other fields, and they need to pursue opportunities to contribute that experience.

The managerial response to change, in summary, must go beyond looking for the perfect technology—there is none. Nor is there likely to be a slowing of the process of change within the information technology environment in the foreseeable future. The archival manager therefore must be able to accept change as commonplace, to be comfortable with the challenge of preparing his or her organization to deal with change as it occurs, and to create an atmosphere in which change is anticipated rather than feared. The greatest managerial challenges in dealing with technological change are more likely to be cultural than technical.

Suggested Readings

Useful introductions to computers and their archival applications include Margaret Hedstrom, *Archives and Manuscripts: Machine Readable Records* (Chicago: Society of American Archivists, 1983); and Richard Kesner, *Automation for Archivists and Record Managers: Planning and Implementation Strategies* (Chicago: American Library Association, 1984). Much of the last is revised and expanded in Kesner's *Information Systems: A Strategic Approach to Planning and Implementation* (Chicago: American Library Association, 1988). Richard Kesner, ed., *Information Management, Machine Readable Records, and Administration: An Annotated Bibliography* (Chicago: Society of American Archivists, 1983) is aging but indispensable. *Archives and Museum Informatics* (Pittsburgh: Archives and Museum Informatics) is a welcome addition to the literature, as is its companion series of *Archives and Museum Informatics Technical Reports*. Archival managers with an interest in their own or their staff's education in automation and related fields should consult Lisa B. Weber, "Educating Archivists for Automation," *Library Trends* (Winter 1988).

Though written to emphasize the technical rather than the managerial implications of automation, Richard M. Kesner, "Automated Information Management: Is There a Role for the Archivist in the Office of the Future?" *Archivaria* 19 (Winter 1984-1985) should interest any archival manager. Written by noted futurist and consultant John Diebold, *Business in the Age of Information* (New York: AMACOM, 1985) has some interesting projections.

Management Literature
and
Professional Associations

The following essay is provided as an introduction to management literature and to a wide range of professional associations. Briefly, professional associations range from academic organizations dealing with theoretical issues with little immediate impact on the working manager to those with a more practical mission. Not surprisingly, the periodical literature reflects this spectrum.

Archival and Related Associations

Professional associations within the archives, records management, and library worlds tend to focus on what this manual has referred to as technical management rather than institutional management, that is, they are more concerned with the care of records and other materials than with the acquisition and use of resources. Nevertheless, these organizations recognize institutional management as a valid professional concern and sponsor journals and other publications, as well as conferences and workshops, pertaining to management and related topics. A partial list of such organizations follows.

- The Society of American Archivists (SAA)
  600 S. Federal, Suite 504
  Chicago, Illinois 60605

- National Association of Government Archivists
  and Records Administrators (NAGARA)
  c/o New York State Archives
  Albany, New York 12230

- American Records Management Association (ARMA)
  4200 Somerset, Suite 215
  Prairie Village, Kansas 66208

- American Association for State and Local History (AASLH)
  172 Second Avenue, North, Suite 103
  Nashville, Tennessee 37201

- American Association of Museums (AAM)
  1225 "I" Street, N.W., Suite 200
  Washington, D.C. 20005

- American Library Association (ALA)
  50 E. Huron
  Chicago, Illinois 60611

A list of regional archival organizations may be obtained by writing SAA at the above address.

Within SAA, the focal point for management issues is the Management Roundtable, which, among other activities, publishes a newsletter containing book reviews and other features of interest to the archival manager.

Professional Management Associations

The Encyclopedia of Associations (Detroit: Gale Research, 1987) lists over twenty-three thousand national and international organizations, with several thousand of these devoted in some way or another to business, management, or the management of various technologies. Those noted below are but a sample.

Academy of Management (Mississippi State University, Mississippi State, Mississippi 39762)—Membership in the academy includes academic professionals in business, management science, and related disciplines, as well as corporate executives selected on the basis of their contributions to management literature. The academy publishes the *Academy of Management Review*, with a strong theoretical and conceptual thrust, and the *Academy of Management Journal*, which attempts to put some emphasis on applications.

American Management Associations (135 W. 50th Street, New York, New York 10020)—This organization is very active in publishing and promoting workshops and conferences. AMA's focus is on the working manager, rather than on the academic pursuit of management science. Many of AMA's efforts are directed specifically at the professional-turned-manager.

American Society for Public Administration (Suite 500, 1120 "G" Street, N.W., Washington, D.C. 20005)—While many of the groups described here offer programs and literature of use to managers in both the for-profit and not-for-profit sectors, ASPA focuses on the latter. In fact, ASPA has been an important factor in the development of professional standards and educational programs in the field of public administration.

Association for Information and Image Management (1100 Wayne Avenue, Suite 1100, Silver Spring, Maryland 20910)—Organized in the 1930s as the National Microfilm Association, it later evolved into the National Micrographics Association to encompass changes in microform techniques. Its latest transformation results from the advent of optical/digital storage devices. AIIM is an aggressive promoter of the combined meeting and trade show, complete with multi-track workshops on techniques and applications.

Association for Systems Management (24587 Bagley Road, Cleveland, Ohio 44138)—Numerous associations have sprung up over the last two decades to deal with the computer and its various applications. ASM seems to have carved out a useful niche for itself by dealing with the managerial implications of computers and related technologies in language that can be understood by the nontechnician.

Society for Advancement of Management (2331 Victory Parkway, Cincinnati, Ohio 45206)— Though retaining academic ties, SAM is directed toward practical applications and runs an active program of workshops and conferences directed toward the needs of the working manager.

Periodical Literature

Since management for the information professional today encompasses both traditional managerial topics (personnel, finance, etc.) and the management of technology, journals on both are noted below.

Harvard Business Review—HBR remains a useful publication for several reasons, among them, its broad range of topics (How many journals would likely publish articles by Mikhail Gorbachev and T. Boone Pickens in the same issue?) and a continuing editorial emphasis on the writing ability of its contributors. Beyond Messrs. Gorbachev and Pickens, *HBR* achieves a comfortable balance between corporate, public, and academic contributors and topics.

Journal of Systems Management—Published by the Association for Systems Management, *JSM* is a well-edited publication focusing on the applications and implications of technology. *JSM* tends toward the view that computers and related technologies are tools, not magic boxes, and that ill-used tools can be worse than no tools at all. The editors appear to make a determined effort to keep jargon from their pages, to the point that most acronyms do not appear without full expansion. This may appear a small point, but not all technical publications are equally considerate.

Management Review—Published by the American Management Associations in a magazine format, *Management Review* offers at least a few items of interest to the public sector manager in almost every issue. Features include some very good regular or aperiodic columns by experts in various fields.

Management Solutions—Also published by AMA, *Management Solutions* emphasizes brief, popularized articles focusing primarily on supervisory issues. (Not surprisingly, it was formerly published under the title *Supervisory Management*.) This is a fairly entertaining publication, which runs case study features in which readers are invited to submit their opinions for publication in a later issue.

Personnel Journal—The personnel field offers a wealth of valuable publications, including *Personnel Journal*. Also useful and readable are *Personnel* and (on a more scholarly level) *Human Resources Management*.

Public Administration Review—Published by the American Society for Public Administration, *PAR* has long been an important source in its field. Public administration has encountered many of the same problems confronted by the archival profession, e.g., education, the need for research, etc., and archivists might find the literature on these issues of great interest.

SAM Advanced Management Journal—Somewhat more focused than *HBR*, with emphasis on improving management techniques, the Society for the Advancement of Management's *Advanced Management Journal* frequently builds its issues around a single topic. Recent numbers have included such themes as "Employee Development and Productivity," and "Strategic Planning and Training."

Other Periodical Sources—As noted above, the archival, records management, and library publications include articles dealing with management or related topics. *Library Journal*'s regular feature "How Do You Manage?" is both entertaining and useful. "Business" magazines, such as *Forbes, Business Week,* and *Fortune,* concentrate on the private sector (and on profit centers even there), but occasionally run pieces of general interest, as do the business sections of major newspapers. Peter Drucker's editorial columns in the *Wall Street Journal* are generally perceptive and provocative. Citations to individual articles listed below should give leads to other journals that may be of value.

Books and Articles

In addition to books and articles cited below, readers should consult the Suggested Readings notes following each chapter and occasional bibliographic footnotes.

The library profession has produced a small but useful collection of management literature, much of which can be applied to the archival profession. Works of interest include:

Bommer, Michael R. W., and Ronald W. Chorba. *Decision Making for Library Management.* White Plains, N.Y.: Knowledge Industry Publications, 1982. (This is one volume in the Professional Librarian Series. Other volumes in this series are also worth reviewing.)

Rizzo, John R. *Management for Librarians.* Westport, Conn.: Greenwood Press, 1980.

* * *

General

Drucker, Peter. *The Frontiers of Management: Where Tomorrow's Decisions Are Being Shaped Today.* New York: Truman Talley, 1986.
_____. *The Practice of Management.* New York: Harper and Row, 1954.

Miner, John B. *Introduction to Management.* Columbus, Ohio: Merrill, 1985.

Odiorne, George S. *How Managers Make Things Happen.* Englewood Cliffs, N.J.: Prentice-Hall, 1982.

Technology and Management

Bell, Daniel. *The Coming of Post-Industrial Society.* New York: Basic Books, 1976.

Drucker, Peter. *The Age of Discontinuity.* New York: Harper and Row, 1968.
_____. *Technology, Management, and Society.* New York: Harper and Row, 1982.

Tushman, Michael L. *Readings in the Management of Innovation.* Boston: Pitman, 1982.

Computers and Information Systems for Managers

Kerzner, Harold. *Project Management for Executives.* New York: Van Nostrand, 1982.

Organizational Theory and Effectiveness

Daft, Richard L. *Organization Theory and Design.* 2d ed. St. Paul: West Publishing, 1986.

Cameron, Kim. "Critical Questions in Assessing Organizational Effectiveness." *Organizational Dynamics* 9 (Autumn 1980).

Cameron, Kim, and David A. Whetten. *Organizational Effectiveness: A Comparison of Multiple Models.* New York: Academic Press, 1983.

Pennings, Johannes, ed. *Organizational Strategy and Change.* San Francisco: Jossey-Bass, 1985.

Schein, Edgar H. *Organizational Culture and Leadership.* San Francisco: Jossey-Bass, 1985.

Yates, Douglas. *The Politics of Management.* San Francisco: Jossey-Bass, 1985.

Planning

Ackoff, Russell L. *A Concept of Corporate Planning.* New York: Wiley, 1970.

Hussey, David E. *Corporate Planning: Theory and Practice.* 2d ed. New York: Pergamon Press, 1982.

Index